Dear my
Forever —
for us girls on our
journey! Love you,
Marla

PRAISE FOR *DEAL WITH IT!*

"I believe Paula White is on the cutting edge of what God is saying now; not what God *was* saying, not what God *will* say—she's dealing with the right-now things of what God *is* saying. This is a woman that the world needs to hear."

—BISHOP T. D. JAKES
Founder and Senior Pastor of The Potter's House

"She has done it again! Paula White has broken life's issues down to the lowest common denominator and delivered a liberating message of hope through Jesus Christ."

—REVEREND BERNICE KING
Daughter to Rev. Martin Luther King Jr.

"Paula White is an excellent teacher of God's word. I believe that she can teach you how to confront the issues and overcome hang-ups so that you can be all that God has created you to be."

—JOYCE MEYER
Author of the best-selling book, *Knowing God Intimately*

"Paula White's book deals with real people and real-life issues—with things that people don't talk about, but need to . . . I think *Deal With It!* is going to be life changing."
—DARRYL (Former All-Star, New York Yankees) AND CHARISSE STRAWBERRY

"Paula White is one of the most significant voices in the body of Christ today, who by way of her personal pain has a powerful triumphant message to release you from the bondage of pain in your own life. . . I urge you to . . . open the windows of your soul to the message Paula White is about to release. Yes, you can *Deal With It!*"

—DR. MARK CHIRONNA
Overseer of Master's Touch International Church

"What God has done with Pastors Randy and Paula White is amazing. God is amazing . . . To see what the Lord has done with them is proof that God will do the same with you."

—BENNY HINN
Bestselling author of *Good Morning, Holy Spirit*

"Paula White is the real deal, and *Deal With It!* gives you the tools to deal with those issues that we all want to ignore."

—CINDY THOMAS

"I think the thing I relate to the most about Paula is that she . . . calls it like it is, she doesn't pull punches, and what she says is more than a philosophy—it really works. Pastor Paula's new book, *Deal With It!*, is awesome. It's full of life lessons that are really practical, hard-hitting solutions."

—TAMARA LOWE

"Joni and I love and appreciate Paula White and her anointing. She is an anointed minister of the Gospel, she is a great blessing, and we love and appreciate her and Randy very much. You are going to be so blessed by *Deal With It!* "

—MARCUS AND JONI LAMB
Founders of Daystar Television Network

"I've known Paula White for many years now and I am telling you that the book that she has released, *Deal With It!*, is a book that you must have. It will absolutely show you step by step how you can be an overcomer and how you can win no matter what happens in your life—God is for you!"

—JENTZEN FRANKLIN
Pastor, Free Chapel Worship Center

"Once again, Paula White is teaching us how to be overcomers. It's not what you achieve in life that makes you who you are—it's what you overcome. You need to get *Deal With It!*"

— HARRY AND SHERYL (former Miss America) SALEM

"Paula White is a gift to the body of Christ . . . Her new book, *Deal With It!*, will be a blessing to you, because you cannot conquer what you will not confront. Buy it, and share it with your friends and family."

—DR. FRANK M. REID, III
Sr. Pastor, Bethel House of God

"Paula White is at the forefront of what God is doing on the Earth today. She is a message to this generation . . . *Deal With It!* is going to help you deal with all the problems that you have in your life."

—MELISSA PITTMAN
Wife of Michael Pittman of the Tampa Bay Buccaneers

"Paula White is strength and courage . . . *Deal With It!* is very simple. It teaches you how to deal with issues in life as a wife, as a mother, and as a professional. It's a book for men as well. So men, put down your remote, set the football aside, and pick up this book—it is powerful."

—JUAN AND JANETTE LONG

DEAL
WITH IT!

DEAL
WITH IT!
YOU CANNOT CONQUER WHAT
YOU WILL NOT CONFRONT

PAULA WHITE

OLIVER
NELSON
™

THOMAS NELSON PUBLISHERS®
Nashville

A Division of Thomas Nelson, Inc.
www.ThomasNelson.com

Published in Nashville, Tennessee, by Thomas Nelson, Inc.

All Scripture quotations, unless otherwise indicated, are taken from the New King James Version®. Copyright © 1982 by Thomas Nelson, Inc. Used by permission. All rights reserved.

Scriptures marked KJV are from the King James Version of the Bible.

ISBN: 0-7852-6106-0

Printed in the United States of America

05 06 07 QW 6

First and foremost, thank You, Lord, for Your unfailing love and Your greatness. You are amazing! Words will never articulate my love and desire for you.

To my husband, my coach, my best friend and covenant partner, Randy, who encourages and inspires me to be all that God has destined for me. You are a rare gem that becomes more valuable each day. My love for you is indescribable.

To my four children—Bradley, Brandon, Angie and Kristen. You are my joy and motivation. You have my heart! I believe in you and am so proud of you.

To my spiritual father and mother, Bishop T. D. and First Lady Serita Jakes. Your wisdom and guidance have been invaluable and have helped mold me and navigate the destiny of my life. I honor you and love you.

To the staff of Paula White Ministries and Without Walls International Church. Thank you for faithfully serving the Lord and your diligence to bring the vision to pass. Great will be your reward.

To my extended family and friends, whom I love and appreciate.

And to my World Partners. Without you, Paula White Ministries would not be what it is today. Thank you for believing in a "messed up Mississippi girl" with a big God and a big dream. Together we are transforming lives, healing hearts and saving souls.

CONTENTS

CONTENTS

YOU CANNOT CONQUER WHAT
YOU WILL NOT CONFRONT

Mirror, mirror, on the wall . . .
Most of us grew up knowing the conclusion to that line from a children's fairy tale. We all, of course, want the mirror to answer us, *"You* are the fairest of them all!" Or if not the fairest, at least the smartest, richest, most capable, famous, powerful, talented, important . . . or spiritual.

But what does the mirror *really* say?

What does the mirror of the *soul* really reflect back to us?

This book is based on a premise:

You can't conquer what you will not confront.

And you can't confront what you don't identify.

Each of us bears the responsibility for looking into the mirrors of our own souls and *dealing* with what we see there.

If you are unwilling to identify, and then confront, the major issues of life, you can't be truly successful in the eyes of the Lord and obtain the destiny full of promise and provision that He has for you. You cannot live a joyful, purposeful, fulfilling life of destiny unless you identify and confront anything that would keep you from being successful in His eyes.

I certainly know that to be true in my personal life.

Many years ago when I first met my husband, Randy, I found myself struggling with those "is he the one?" questions. Randy hadn't seemed at all my "type" when we first met, but the more I got to know him, the more I liked him. We began to date, and I soon realized I was falling in love with him.

At that point, I began to put up a wall in my heart. *Be careful!* my heart said. *If he gets to know the real you, he'll reject you just like all the others have!* Subconsciously even more than consciously, I concluded, *Don't let him hurt you! If you let him get any closer or discover any more about you, he'll walk out.*

Old hurts and emotions from my childhood and teen years began to bubble up and I felt myself instinctively to be in danger of being exposed, injured, and abandoned. So I did what I had always done when I found myself with those feelings—I began to try to manipulate the relationship to my advantage.

There was only one problem. Randy, unlike every man I had known before him, refused to be manipulated!

One evening we quarreled over something I had done, and when Randy confronted me about it, I began to pull out all of my same old excuses and defenses. Randy further confronted me about my manipulative behavior, and a heated discussion degenerated into an all-out argument. The more I felt myself losing ground, the higher the wall rose inside me and the more I resorted to my usual "techniques."

When theatrical speaking and gesturing failed, I fell to the floor, pulled my knees to my chest in a fetal position, and cried my own brand of crocodile tears. I punctuated my words with great gasps of air and heaving sobs. I was fully prepared to hyperventilate if necessary as I screamed out the bits and phrases of my well-rehearsed role, "You don't know! You don't understand! Your daddy didn't commit suicide! You were never abused!"

I was certain Randy would reach down and wrap his strong arms around me to comfort me. I was confident he would hold me and stroke me in sympathy, and that we would eventually get to the kiss-and-make-up stage.

But Randy didn't do any of what I expected.

Long, slow, agonizing seconds turned into a minute . . . then two. Finally I opened one eye and slightly lifted my head to see if he was still in the room. He was.

Randy was standing several feet away, staring at me with a stern look on his face. His words were not at all the ones I had anticipated—or the ones I felt sure I would hear as I silently pleaded with him using a "pity-me" gaze.

Rather, Randy said simply and strongly, "When you want to act like an adult and talk to me . . . then we'll talk. When you're ready to deal with this in a rational way . . . call me."

And he walked out.

I cried even louder, but he didn't come back. I paced the floor and my self-pity turned to anger. How could he be so unsympathetic? How could he be so cold? How could he treat me that way?

After a couple of hours of fuming and weeping, I crawled into bed, thinking, *Surely he'll call me.*

But he didn't.

We had been having dinner together almost every night. *Surely he'll show up for dinner with a bouquet of my favorite flowers,* I thought.

But he didn't.

We had been talking four or five times on most days, and every time the phone rang, I was sure he was on the other end of the line, ready to apologize and sympathize.

But no call came.

Two days passed . . . then three, five, eight . . . and finally ten days. I decided I could be just as stubborn as he was. Eleven, twelve, thirteen, fourteen days. No call. No note in the mailbox. No contact. Finally, I sat before my mirror in the bathroom and stared long and hard at the sad, tear-drained person staring back at me. I took a long, hard look at myself—not just at my appearance, but at my life.

What was the problem?

Who had the problem?

What was the solution?

Who had the answer?

I picked up the phone and called Randy. He answered with a very pleasant, "Oh, I see you're ready to act like an adult. You're ready to *deal with this*. Now we can work through it."

The two weeks of silence between us had seemed like an eternity. I was glad we were back in communication, but deep inside, I also knew that I had monumental issues I needed to address. But how? Where should I turn? What should I do?

I finally picked up my Bible and held it up to the Lord. I said, "Lord, I don't want to be going around this mountain when I'm forty or fifty years old. I don't want to be on my third or fourth marriage, facing the same issues and hurts deep in my soul. Help me!"

I began to diligently dissect my Bible, and especially the women of the Bible. They became my mentors, my role models. I discovered that the women of the Bible also had faced very serious issues, and that in their lives they had discovered some very important principles and had gained some very important answers.

What I learned from them, I trust you will also learn from them.

If you are willing to identify, confront, and conquer the issues of your life— to truly *deal with them*—God will heal you, restore you, and lead you into the destiny that He has planned for you, a destiny that is beyond your wildest dreams.

DEAL
WITH IT!

∽ GOD'S WORD ON RUTH

Ruth was a Moabitess. She grew up on the high plateau south of the Arnon River, during the time of the Israelite judges, as part of a nation that worshipped the false god Chemosh. She married into a Hebrew family that came to Moab from Bethlehem to escape a famine. Naomi was Ruth's mother-in-law. After the husbands of both Naomi and Ruth died, Naomi decided to return to Bethlehem. Ruth refused to be left behind. She went with Naomi to Bethlehem and began a new life. She worked in the barley fields of Naomi's relative Boaz, gleaning the edges of the grain field. She eventually won the respect and love of Boaz, who took her as his wife. The Scripture reference for Ruth's story is Ruth 1:16–22, and you will find it in the Appendix to this book.

1

RUTH

"A person with my background just can't succeed."

Apart from the unnamed woman in Proverbs 31, Ruth is the only woman in the Bible who is called a "virtuous woman." That wasn't, however, a description that came from her early years.

Ruth was born and raised in Moab, and the Moabites worshipped a god by the name of Chemosh. Part of this very lewd form of worship involved the sacrifice of young children to Chemosh as an offering (see 2 Kings 3:27). The mentality of all the Moabite people was distorted by this idolatry. A society that sacrifices young children is a society that has very little value for life or family. We can conclude from the atmosphere of her childhood and teenage years that Ruth was exposed to a highly perverse culture and the worst forms of human behavior.

Moab was considered a "cursed" place by the Jewish people. Centuries before, Abraham's nephew, Lot, had escaped Sodom with his two daughters. Lot's wife looked back and became a pillar of salt. Lot and his two daughters managed to hide out in the mountains after Sodom and Gomorrah were destroyed by fire and brimstone. The daughters, no doubt thinking that they and their father were the only three people left alive on the entire earth, got their father drunk on two successive nights. They each had sex with their father and they each became pregnant by him. One of the children born

3

out of this incest was named Moab. His descendants were the Moabites.

Because of the sin in which he was born, Moab and the nation that he produced was "accursed." God's Word tells us that there was no dancing, no praise, no gladness in the fields, and no joy in the streets of Moab because it was a cursed place. The Bible says this about Moab: "'Fear and the pit and the snare shall be upon you, O inhabitant of Moab,' says the LORD" (Jer. 48:43).

Can you imagine what it might have been like to grow up in this lifeless, idolatrous, sorrow-filled place? Those who worship idols are always disappointed and bitter to some degree because no idol can give a person life or blessing or a future. The idol worshiper invariably has to come face-to-face with the fact that he is worshipping a self-made, dead, lifeless god. What could be more sorrowful than taking the body of a dead child from before the altar of a dead god? A spirit of death hung over Moab, Ruth's homeland. She grew up under the oppression of that spirit. Her upbringing was very different from that of the man she married.

Ruth became the wife of Chilion, the son of Elimelech and Naomi. Elimelech was a Jewish farmer who had come to Moab with his wife and two sons to escape a severe famine that had brought all of Judah to the point of starvation. Elimelech and Naomi were from Bethlehem. Both of their sons—Mahlon and Chilion—married Moabite girls. The older son married a woman named Orpah. The younger son married Ruth.

Now, it was acceptable in Moab for a Moabite girl to marry a Jewish boy, but it was *not* acceptable in the Jewish tradition for a Jewish boy to marry a Moabite girl. Even if nothing was said out in the open, there had to have been an undercurrent in that home that something "wasn't quite right."

Mahlon and Chilion were apparently prone to sickness. Mahlon's name means "puny"—he may have been born prematurely. Chilion's name means "unhealthy." Both of these men died young. Elimelech also died. Naomi found herself a widow with two widowed daughters-in-law.

Ruth, who had lived under the shadow of death all her life, had encountered even more death. She who had known the bitterness and disappointment that are part of idol worship now found herself living with a mother-in-law who was bitter and disappointed.

All of these things must have played a part in making Ruth who she was. Experiences such as the ones she had, and the atmosphere of the environment in which she lived, must have had an impact on her psyche. We can say that our environment doesn't impact us, or that the comments of other people don't have an influence on us, but deep inside, we know that isn't true.

In the light of her past and the events of her present, there was something great about Ruth—she rose above her past. She had an ability to look at her past and present and say, "I want no more of this. I want something better. I want something more."

After the death of the men in this family, Naomi heard that the famine was over in Bethlehem, and she decided to return home. She began her journey with both of her daughters-in-law by her side, but along the way, she stopped and told them to turn around and go back to Moab—to return to their people and their gods. One daughter-in-law agreed and returned. But Ruth loved Naomi and "clung to her" (Ruth 1:14).

Naomi said to these young women, "Go back to your families. Go back to the customs and ways in which you were raised. I'm going to a place that is unfamiliar to you."

Ruth refused to return and said, "Your people shall be my people, and your God, my God" (Ruth 1:16). Ruth wanted the customs and traditions and God of Naomi. She was saying to her, "I'm going where I've never been to create something I've never had . . . because in knowing you, Naomi, I've come to love you. I've come to know your God and love your God. I'm willing to go where I have never been to become something I want to be."

Ruth recognized that she had already experienced her past, and she hadn't liked it. There was nothing left that had any value to her. She made a choice.

Millions of people are where Ruth was in that moment. They each have a past they wish they could forget. They've already experienced their pasts, and what they experienced brought them nothing but pain and heartache. They see nothing of value in the pasts they've lived.

Are you there?

Is your past one that you wish you had never lived?

Is your past something that you want to continue to relive again and again?

You cannot enter your tomorrow as long as you hold on to your past. You must let go.

This is often easier said than done. For many of us, our pasts hold brokenness, disappointment, and scars from life's tragedies, and we are still living out the consequences of our failures and foolish choices. You might think that letting go of the bad things in the past would be easy—yet often in a twisted, distorted way, we hold on to our pasts because they are something with which we are familiar. There's a sense of security in holding on to the familiar . . . even if the familiar is bad.

Often we are afraid to enter the future because it is unknown and unfamiliar. Even though it may be much better than our past, we haven't been there yet. It isn't what we're used to. Therefore, we drag the past into our future because we feel more comfortable being abased than we do abounding. As long as we do this, we can never be free from the past.

What about you?

Are you ready to let go of your past? Are you ready to give it a graveyard burial and not resurrect it?

Are you ready to move forward into the future God has for you?

Your tomorrow does not have to be like your yesterday. Where you came from doesn't determine where you are going!

Too many people today are predicting their endings based on their beginnings. In life the most important thing is not where you start, but where you finish. I am so thankful that God can interrupt a person's life and change the course of history for that person for His good. God does not use your past to determine your future . . . so why should you? It's a tragedy to plan your future by comparing it to your past. Stop using what *was* to determine what *will be!*

LEAVING YOUR PAST

Ruth made a decision to leave her past, and it was the most important decision of her life. It's one of the most important decisions *you* can make.

Most people don't move beyond their upbringing.

Most people don't go beyond the socioeconomic barriers of their parents.

Most people don't go beyond what they have been exposed to in their pasts. Most people don't break out of their ethnicities or cultures.

Why was Ruth willing to leave what was familiar? What caused her to embrace an unknown future and leave behind a well-known past?

A DELIBERATE AND CONSCIOUS ACT

As a child who was sexually and physically abused, I developed forms of behavior that were abnormal and "sick" to a normal person, but they were comfortable and familiar behaviors to me. At the time, I did not have the ability to move beyond those behaviors as a child being raised in an ungodly home. It takes a very deliberate conscious act on the part of an adult to confront old familiar habits developed in childhood and move beyond them to wholeness. It is a choice that you must make.

Leaving the past behind does not mean that we only leave the negative aspects of the past behind. For some people, the struggle is in leaving behind a past that they perceive to be better than their present. There are some people who have trouble letting go of past success. They might be fifty years old with lots of cellulite and a hundred extra pounds, but they are still putting on the tiara and remembering the days when they were prom queen. Or they create a fantasized past and dwell in a set of false memories. The past—no matter what it is—needs to be left in the past!

"Leave and cleave" is a Bible principle that applies to every person. You must leave your past and cleave to what God has for you.

Leave your yesterday . . . and cleave to today.

Leave your failures . . . and cleave to God's promises.

Leave your old sin . . . and cleave to the forgiveness God gives you.

The truth is, you can't look backward and forward at the same time. If you try to move forward while looking backward, you'll be highly unstable. You won't keep your balance and you'll fail. Jesus said, "No one, having put his hand to the plow, and looking back, is fit for the kingdom of God" (Luke 9:62). To be "fit" means to be appropriate or qualified. The kingdom of God is God's system, the royal realm of God. If you do your work while looking over your shoulder to your past all the time, you won't be qualifying yourself for the royal future God has for you.

A CONTINUAL PROCESS

Leaving your yesterdays is a continual process. You don't just "leave" the past once and for all. You leave yesterday behind the moment you begin today. As you move into tomorrow, you leave behind the today that has become a yesterday. With every step forward, there must be a leaving of what is past.

Stepping into the promise of your potential is always a matter of stepping out of your past.

Let me share with you five things about your past and your future:

1. *God does not consult your past to determine your future.* Everybody has a "past" of some kind—a past that God expects us to leave behind. The book of Joshua reminds us that even Abraham and his family "dwelt on the other side of the River in old times" and "served other gods" (see Joshua 24:2). Even the man who was chosen by God to become the father of all who have faith, had a "past."

God does not consult your past to determine your future.

God does not bind you to your past.

A number of people told Randy not to marry me. They said, "She's not 'ministry material.'" I didn't play the piano. I didn't look like or dress like a preacher's wife. I didn't come from a Christian upbringing. I used to say to people, "Randy was from five generations of preachers, while I was from five generations of heathens."

My father committed suicide when I was five years old.

I was sexually and physically abused from the age of six to thirteen.

I never heard the gospel until I was eighteen years old.

Family gave up on me; friends gave up on me; psychiatrists gave up on me . . . but God never gave up on me.

After I was saved at the age of eighteen, God gave me a vision. He let me see myself standing before masses of people, and everywhere my voice was heard, multitudes were saved, healed, and delivered. Where my voice was not heard, people were falling off into utter darkness. He spoke in my spirit, *I have called you to preach the gospel.*

For many years, although I knew God had supernaturally called me, I struggled with pursuing that call because of my background.

One night Randy and I were at dinner with a leader in a holiness pentecostal group, and as we were talking with this man about ministry, he said to me, "Paula, God knew every mistake you would ever make. He knew everything you would go through. He knew everything that would happen to you. And He chose to call you. Who is man to override the decision of God?"

Those few words began to set me free. If God, who is omniscient (all-knowing)—fully knowing all of my experiences and all my mistakes—chose to call me, who was I to back away from that call? I could be free of the opinion of man! I could begin to believe that yesterday is in the tomb, tomorrow is in the womb, and what we are intimate with right now is what we will birth in our future.

2. *God commands you to leave your past and press toward the future He has for you.* You must let go of your past to embrace your future. The apostle Paul wrote, "I do not count myself to have apprehended; but one thing I do, forgetting those things which are behind and reaching forward to those things which are ahead, I press toward the goal for the prize of the upward call of God in Christ Jesus" (Phil. 3:13–14).

- *Forgetting.* I had to make a decision to "forget" the things behind. Forgetting does not mean that I developed amnesia. I still have a memory about the tragic events I've experienced. But . . . I choose not to dwell on those memories. I choose not to rethink those same sickening thoughts that once led me into depression. I choose not to think about the times when I was locked in a closet as a child. God's Word tells us, "As he thinks in his heart, so is he" (Prov. 23:7). Our thoughts become our words. Our words become our actions. Our actions become our habits. Our habits become our character. And our character becomes our destiny. You must *choose* to forget and leave the past behind.

- *Reaching Forward.* A part of "reaching forward" is thinking new thoughts. God's Word says, "Whatever things are true, whatever things are noble, whatever things are just, whatever things are pure, whatever things are lovely, whatever things are of good report, if there is any virtue and if there is anything praiseworthy—meditate on these things. The things which you learned and received and heard and saw in me, these do, and the God of peace will be with you" (Phil. 4:8–9). I have to consciously and purposefully choose to think about things that are true, noble, just, pure, lovely, of good report, and praiseworthy.

- *Pressing Toward the Goal.* Paul wrote, "I press toward the goal." To press is to resist that which would hinder your moving into your destiny. Every time a negative thought and feeling about the past rises up, you must say, "I resist the tendency to think this way and feel this way. I choose instead to think new thoughts and to meditate on those things that are praiseworthy. I choose to put the focus on the goal—the prize of an upward call of God in Christ Jesus."

When thoughts about the brokenness of the past come, we must resist them and press toward wholeness.

When thoughts about past losses come—thoughts about things we may have lost materially or relationships we may have lost—we must resist those thoughts and press toward the future blessings God has for us.

A person who is pressing forward has to resist all forms of fear, including the fear of the unknown. One who is pressing forward is moving against the enemy of his or her soul, who is doing his utmost to keep that person from entering the fullness of life that God has promised.

Paul made it very clear that he had not yet arrived. And who has? Not one of us has arrived at the perfection that God holds out to us—the full character likeness of Jesus Christ. But Paul also stated that there was one thing that was imperative for him to do in order to go forward in his life toward perfection. He must forget the past. He must let go of all his yesterdays. Whether yesterday was good or bad, he had to release it.

- *Do not look behind.* Don't long for things that are past. Don't linger mentally, emotionally, or spiritually on those things that are over. Look ahead to where God is leading you!

- *Don't stay anywhere on the plain.* Don't stay on the same level. God wants to take you up to the next level—to the mountains!

In the book of Revelation we read how John was in the Spirit on the Lord's Day and a voice spoke to him saying, "Come up here, and I will show you things which must take place after this" (4:1). God speaks to us about our past and present while we are living on the "plain," but there are some things about your future that God will not reveal to you unless you are willing to leave your past behind and go to a higher level in your relationship with Him.

Genesis 13:14–17 tells us that the Lord said to Abram *after Lot had separated from him,* "Lift your eyes now and look from the place where you are—northward, southward, eastward, and westward: for all the land which you see I give to you and your descendants forever. And I will make your descendants as the dust of the earth; so that if a man could number the dust of the earth, then your descendants also could be numbered. Arise, walk in the land through its length and its width, for I give it to you."

This tremendous promise of God about the land and Abram's descendants was not given to him as long as his nephew Lot was with him. Lot represented Abraham's *past*. Lot also represented disobedience. God had told Abram, "Get out of your country, from your family and from your father's house, to a land that I will show you" (Gen. 12:1). Abram should never have taken Lot with him. Lot was part of Abram's "father's house." He was supposed to cut himself away from his crazy kinfolk and trust God.

Now, God wasn't speaking against family ties. God was calling Abram to break away from the family *mentality*—the mind-set that was still back in Ur of the Chaldeans, thinking about strange gods. Lot was an ever-present reminder of who Abram used to be, what Abram used to do, and what Abram used to believe. It was only *after* those ties were fully broken that God could reveal to Abram the extent of the call and blessing He had for him.

There are some things that God cannot speak into your life until you are willing to separate yourself from your past.

Lift up your eyes!

God tells us that He will not pull us out of our situations, but He will give us a new position, a new vision, a new perspective in our situations. There's blessing all around you, but you can't see it as long as your eyes are focused on your past.

My mother remarried when I was nine years old. She married a man who was a two-star admiral, a very successful man. My mother went on to get two master's degrees, worked toward her doctorate, and she was very successful in hospital administration.

I've lived something of a roller-coaster life. The life I had until my father's suicide when I was five years old was not the life I knew from the ages of six to ten, and that was not the life I knew from the ages of ten to eighteen.

I've known the pits and I've known the palace.

My mother and stepfather were very liberal. They never said,

"Don't have sex" or "Don't drink." They told me that if I was going to have sex, to make sure I loved the person and protected myself. They taught me that if I was going to drink, don't drive. They wanted me to do the safe thing, and the successful thing in the eyes of the world.

After I was saved, I felt that I had an obligation to witness to them and lead them to God. I was very aggressive in my sharing of the gospel with them. My stepfather finally said to me, "I don't want to hear any more about Jesus. If you insist on talking about God in this house, you aren't welcome here."

I had a choice to make. I could stay . . . or leave. I knew that I had to leave, and I did. I had to let go of the past and to embrace a future with God. I had just been saved and I was *beginning* to know God, but I really didn't know God very well at that time. In many ways, I was like Ruth.

To have stayed with my family would have been to stay in Moab. A choice to stay and be quiet about Jesus was a choice to become part of a well-to-do, highly educated, socially liberal, anti-God world.

To leave my family meant to go to Bethlehem—to seek to make a new way and to establish new patterns for my life.

I don't know what your Moab is, but every person has something he or she must leave to follow Jesus completely.

I don't know precisely where your Bethlehem is or who your Boaz is, but God has a place and a purpose for you if you are willing to leave your past and walk into your future *with Him.* As a result of my obedience and willingness to leave my past, today my family is saved and reconciled to God. It did not happen overnight, but God is faithful to fulfill all His promises when you obey Him.

3. *God* always *has a future for you.* God's Word gives us this wonderful promise of the Lord: "For I know the thoughts that I think

toward you, says the LORD, thoughts of peace and not of evil, to give you a future and a hope. Then you will call upon Me and go and pray to Me, and I will listen to you. And you will seek Me and find Me, when you search for Me with all your heart" (Jer. 29:11–13). Ruth was willing to seek the God of Naomi. She was willing to believe for a future and a hope, even though there was nothing that could be considered a basis for that hope other than sheer faith.

Ruth did not have any hope of marriage and children in following Naomi to Bethlehem. She would have had a much better chance of being given in marriage to someone if she had returned to her family in Moab. Naomi spelled that out clearly to her. She said, "I don't have any sons you can marry, and I never will have—and even if I did, you wouldn't want to wait to marry them." Ruth wasn't following Naomi because she knew there was a man in her future. She followed Naomi out of her love and her belief that the God of Naomi was the One who was worthy of her worship.

Nevertheless, she was looking toward Bethlehem. She was walking toward Bethlehem. She was entering into Bethlehem.

Focus on your future. What you focus on is what captures your attention and your affection.

4. *Change your focus.* You must change your focus as you leave your past and embrace your future. You must begin to see yourself in new ways.

There's no room in your future for a "victim mentality." People with a victim mentality are people who say, "I can't get out until you let me out," "I can't be happy until you make me happy," or "I can't succeed until you allow me to succeed." People with a victim mentality give away all power to other people!

God never leaves your destiny in anyone else's hands. God never intends for you to give away the authority and power of your own life. God's Word tells us that if you speak the Word, think the Word, and do the Word, your way will be prosperous—then you will be successful (see Joshua 1:8). It doesn't depend on what other people do. It depends on what *you* do.

You are a victor, not a victim.

People who are close to me know that I don't particularly prefer Father's Day. It's a meaningless day for me since I don't know what it means to have the lifelong love of a father, to be twirled around as his little girl, to sit in a daddy's lap and cry over a lost boyfriend, or to be escorted by a father to a prom. But I don't live in Father's Day. There are 364 other days of the year! I live in the fullness of what God has given to me—a husband who loves me; children who bring great joy to me and are saved; a wonderful ministry; and blessings all around me.

I don't place great emphasis on the fact that I didn't have a father in my life. I emphasize what I *do* have and have been given. What you look at longest is what will become strongest in your life. Whatever captures your attention, masters you.

Choose to put your focus on the *good* things God has done for you, is doing for you, and will do for you.

5. *Prepare yourself in the Word.* You must begin to prepare yourself for what is coming. Anything significant and positive that happens in your life is something that *you* must initiate by the Word of God—speaking the Word, thinking and meditating upon the Word, and doing the Word. If you are going to fully embrace your future, you must embrace what the Word of God has to say about you.

The ant is a forward thinker. Proverbs 6:6 tells us, "Go to the ant, you sluggard! Consider her ways and be wise." What does the ant do? "Having no captain, overseer or ruler," the ant "provides her supplies in the summer and gathers her food in the harvest" (vv. 8–9). The ant prepares for its own future.

Two of the most powerful words you can speak are these: *"I'm *preparing.*" The moment you say, "I'm preparing," you send notice to the world, the devil, and your past. You are saying, "I'm going somewhere!"

To prepare is to make "cuts" in your life that put you in alignment with the pattern of what is yet to be. When you prepare a length of cloth to become a piece of clothing, you cut the cloth according to the pattern of the garment you intend to sew. We are to bring our lives in alignment with what the Word of God says about us—that's the pattern for our lives.

Get into the Word.

Study the Word.

Memorize the Word.

Speak the Word.

Meditate on the Word.

Act on the Word.

REFUSE TO CARRY BITTERNESS INTO YOUR FUTURE

In making a decision to leave Moab and go to Bethlehem, Ruth was also making a decision to serve Naomi. Her decision was a conscious decision to serve because Naomi was not an easy person to love at that time.

Naomi's experiences in Moab had left her hard and cynical. She was angry about the death of her husband and sons (see Ruth 1:20–21). When her old friends came out to greet her as she arrived in Bethlehem, they called her name, "Naomi! Naomi!" She said, "Don't call me Naomi"—which means "pleasant." She told them, "Call me Mara"—which means bitter. Naomi was blaming God for what had happened to her.

It isn't easy to serve a bitter person, but Ruth made that decision. Why?

Because Ruth knew to whom she had been assigned.

Almost no one in today's world seems to know or accept what it means to be "assigned" to serve another person. The prophet Elisha knew that he had been assigned to serve and learn under the prophet Elijah. The disciples of Jesus knew that they had been called to serve and learn under Jesus. My husband, Randy, and I knew for five years that we were to serve and learn from Dr. Lowery. We knew our "assignment."

When you know that you have been assigned by God to serve and learn from someone, you are willing to put up with all kinds of difficulties that come to distract you from that relationship. You are willing to do all kinds of jobs and put up with all kinds of hardships because you know without a doubt that God has called you to that relationship to teach you, prepare you, and ultimately, to bless you for your obedience.

If God has assigned you to somebody, serve that person and learn from him . . . willingly! Do it gladly and with joy. Do it faithfully and with humility. God is preparing you for something greater than you can imagine!

THE NATURE OF BITTERNESS

Countless people are bitter today because of what they think God has done to them.

In reality, of course, Naomi shouldn't have blamed God for what had happened. God had not called Elimelech and Naomi to go to Moab. In fact, the command of God to all the Israelites was just the opposite—*don't* go to Moab. In going to Moab, Elimelech had both failed to trust God and had disobeyed God. The consequences he and his family suffered were consequences of his own actions.

There are always consequences for disobedience, *even if you don't know that you are disobeying*. People say, "But I didn't know it was wrong," as if that's going to wipe away all consequences for their sin. It's as if they are saying, "But I didn't know about gravity," as they step off a ten-story ledge. The consequences of sin always come in some form of death. God's Word is very clear on that: "The wages of sin is death" (Rom. 6:23). Sin "pays out" in the form of death—it might be a physical death or an emotional death. It might be a slow and agonizing death over years and even decades, or it might be instant death. Some part of a person "dies" in the presence of sin. It might be the death of innocence, the death of an ability to trust, the death of joy, the death of an ability to "feel deeply," the death of hope, the death of the ability to cry tears, or the death of an ability to risk being vulnerable.

There's nothing you can do in your own self—your own humanity, out of your own initiative, by your own will or effort—to change the consequences related to sin. *But*—and what an amazing word that is in Romans 6:23, "For the wages of sin is death—*but* the gift of God is eternal life in Christ Jesus our Lord."

But . . . the gift of God.

But . . . the presence of Jesus Christ our Lord.

But . . . the forgiveness of a loving heavenly Father that cleanses and renews and restores.

You may have sinned, *but* the gift of God has come to you. You have been given the gift of God that is eternal life in Christ Jesus our Lord!

Have you received that gift?

Have you accepted the only gift that can address the consequences of your sin?

Have you accepted the gift of *life* that replaces the consequences of death?

I know what a struggle it can be for a person to accept the gift God offers.

For years, I struggled with my own history. I often wondered, can God do anything with a broken person like me? Can God work through a person with a tainted past?

I couldn't quite see what God might be able to do with a "heathen" woman who had not been raised in church, hadn't heard the gospel until she was almost eighteen years old, and had a lifetime of sowing to the flesh prior to that time.

I knew and believed the truth of Galatians 6:7–8: "Do not be deceived, God is not mocked; for whatever a man sows, that he will also reap. For he who sows to his flesh will of the flesh reap corruption, but he who sows to the Spirit will of the Spirit reap everlasting life."

I had reaped a harvest from years of junk. What could God do with me?

I finally found the answer. God's Word declares, "Therefore, if anyone is in Christ, he is a new creation; old things have passed away; behold, all things have become new" (2 Cor. 5:17).

What that verse says is that the moment I came to Jesus, everything "old" passed away, and I became a new person through Christ Jesus. My sins were forgiven, but even better, it was as if I had never committed them in the eyes of God. He not only forgave me, but He forgot about my past. He never brought my past sins up to me or to anyone else. God's Word says:

> He has not dealt with us according to our sins,
> Nor punished us according to our iniquities.
> For as the heavens are high above the earth,
> So great is his mercy toward those who fear Him;
> As far as the east is from the west,
> So far has He removed our transgressions from us.
>
> (Ps. 103:10–12)

The moment I accepted Jesus, everything old passed away from my life. I became a new person through Christ Jesus. My sins were forgiven and forgotten. My past was over. I was cleansed and made new.

God doesn't have any problem in believing the miracle that He does in our lives. *We* are the ones who have trouble believing that we are forgiven. *We* are the ones who have trouble letting go of the past. *We* are the ones who keep reminding ourselves of our past sin and shame. *We* are the ones who refuse to let go of Moab and take the journey to Bethlehem.

Are you ready to walk out of your past and into your future?

Are you ready to lay down the old so you can pick up the new?

There's something in *you* today that is speaking to you, "God has something for me that is greater, healthier, better, finer, holier, . . . more beautiful than what I've known." Pursue that voice and vision of God for your life. It will lead you into a "land flowing with milk and honey," a place of peace and prosperity.

WALKING INTO YOUR FUTURE

Ruth did not move into her destiny in a day. There were three aspects of her character that were a vital part of her receiving the fullness of what God had for her.

1. *Ongoing Work and Productivity.* Ruth did not show up in Bethlehem and expect her destiny to be handed to her on a silver platter the moment she walked into town. So many people today believe that after they are saved, God is going to turn their world upside down overnight. God's Word tells us that we become new creatures the moment we accept Jesus as our Savior, but it does not tell us that we instantly experience a new environment, new circumstances, new situations, or new relationships. There's a walking out and a working out that's our responsibility. We are the ones who have to create and establish a new atmosphere for our lives—an atmosphere that is focused on God and based on His Word. We are the

ones who need to develop new circumstances and new situations that are good in God's eyes. We are the ones who need to form new relationships that are godly, encouraging, and beneficial.

We are the ones who must lay down the old and pick up the new. The Word says, "If indeed you have heard Him and have been taught by Him, as the truth is in Jesus: that you put off, concerning your former conduct, the old man which grows corrupt according to the deceitful lusts, and be renewed in the spirit of your mind, and that you put on the new man which was created according to God, in true righteousness and holiness" (Eph. 4:21–24).

The apostle Paul was very specific on this point. He said very clearly that we are the ones who put off the old man and put on the new man. We are the ones who must "put away" lying, anger, stealing, corrupt words, bitterness, clamor, wrath, evil speaking, and malice. We are the ones who must "put on" a kind, tenderhearted, forgiving nature. We are the ones who must train our mouths to speak only what is "good for necessary edification" and what imparts "grace to the hearers." We are the ones who must labor, "working with [our] hands what is good that [we] may have something to give him who has need." It is our responsibility to stop grieving the Holy Spirit of God and to love and forgive as Christ loves and forgives us (see Ephesians 3:25–32).

God transforms our desires, our character, our nature . . . but we are the ones who must change our *behavior*. We are the ones who must lay down the past and pick up the future, lay down evil and pick up good, lay down what corrupts and pick up what is eternal.

Ruth went into the barley harvest and worked. She didn't crawl into her bed and pout until somebody gave her the desires of her heart. She got busy and worked tirelessly, and it was while she was *working* that she was noticed by Boaz.

Through the years, I've worked with dozens upon dozens of people—in volunteer settings and employment settings. I've discovered that there are two types of people: the diligent, who show up thirty minutes early and stay late and give their best; and those who wander in ten minutes late, spend a great deal of time stirring coffee and talking idly, and leave the minute they think they can slip away unnoticed.

Those who are diligent succeed. Those who aren't, don't.

2. *An Ongoing Obsession with Doing Good.* Ruth served her mother-in-law. That was her assignment and she fulfilled it. The day came when the women of Bethlehem said to Naomi these words about Ruth: "Your daughter-in-law, who loves you, . . . is better to you than seven sons" (Ruth 4:15).

Ruth didn't date the young men of Bethlehem. She was single-minded in her care of Naomi. Every day she brought home something from her gleanings so that Naomi might have the provision she needed. God's Word says, "Be obedient . . . with good will doing service, as to the Lord, and not to men, knowing that whatever good anyone does, he will receive the same from the Lord" (Eph. 6:5, 7–8). In doing good to Naomi, Ruth was putting herself in a position to receive the blessings of God.

The same is true for us. It is as you work and as you seek to do good to others that God puts you in a position to rise. God's Word tells us, "The LORD upholds all who fall, and raises up all who are bowed down" (Ps. 145:14). Ruth may have appeared "bowed down" as she gleaned grain from the field of Boaz, but she was in precisely the *right* position to be raised up by the Lord!

When you stoop over to put a blanket over the sleeping body of a homeless person . . .

When you stoop down to give a hug to a hurting child . . .

When you stoop to assist a person who is weak or sick . . .

When you reach down to give a "hand up" to a person in need . . .

You are in the very position for God to raise you to an even higher place.

No job is too little or too "unimportant" if you are seeking to do good to others.

Shortly after I was saved and I knew that God had called me to serve others, I went to the pastor of my church and said, "Please find a place to use me." He handed me a broom and a mop. I cleaned floors and cleaned floors and cleaned floors. I cleaned floors to the best of my ability and with all diligence. My pastor noticed my faithfulness and came and said, "I want you to take care of the two-year-olds." Now, there's not a lot of gospel that can be preached to two-year-olds in words, but there's a whole lot of gospel that can be preached to little children by the way you touch them, hold them, and care for them when they are crying, hungry, or need a diaper change. I ministered to those two-year-olds to the best of my ability.

The pastor came and gave me a promotion—to the four-year-olds. I studied and prepared to make sure the four-year-olds were learning the gospel in a way they could receive.

Now for more than twenty years I have ministered in what some would call a wilderness—I call it an oasis . . . the inner cities of America. In the heart of Tampa; Washington, D.C.; Los Angeles; and all of the nation, Randy and I have developed programs and ministry geared towards underprivileged children. We have seen the hand of God move mightily as multitudes have not only experienced salvation, but have also been empowered to live the abundant life that Christ died to give us all. In the early years, my economic condition was not much better than those I was ministering to. However, it didn't matter that we were eating government cheese and living in a cheap apartment. We were doing what the Lord had called us to do and it was *good* and it was *work*.

There isn't anything that you should ever consider "beneath" you when it comes to serving other people. *Every* person is worthy of your best.

3. *An Ongoing Following of Instructions.* Ruth listened to what Boaz told her to do. He told her exactly where to glean and how. She did what he said.

Ruth listened to her mother-in-law. She took her instruction and followed it to the letter. Naomi told Ruth exactly what to do to win the affection of Boaz and to motivate him to become her kinsman-redeemer . . . and Ruth did exactly what Naomi told her to do.

When Boaz told her what he was going to do, she listened.

When Naomi told her what to say, she listened.

One of the greatest signs of respect that you can show a person who is in authority over you is to listen closely and then *do* what he or she requests you to do. Learn to follow instructions precisely. Learn to be discreet in asking questions, in respecting the time of your leaders, and in refraining from repeating what they ask you to keep in confidence. In following the instructions of those in authority over you, you are giving them honor, and as you honor them, you honor the Lord who is over them!

At the time I left my parents' house, I was part of a small country church. There were three women in that church who fully embraced me, and they became my mentors. They taught me how to live a godly life by their example. They taught me deep principles about God in the way they gave their tithes, in the way they honored and respected their husbands, in the way they dressed and talked, and in the way they treated other people. We often had all-night prayer meetings together in which we sought God with our whole hearts, minds, and souls. They taught me how to come into the presence of a holy God and to worship Him with total submission and abandonment. They showed me how to be faithful and instructed me in how to live a life that is pleasing to the Lord.

These women did not move in the same social, economic, or educational circles as my parents. They were not as "successful" as my parents according to the standards of the world. But these women moved in the Spirit. They had peace, love, and joy in their lives. They knew how to pray and how to touch God with their faith. They knew how to live out God's Word in their lives. In God's eyes, they were supremely successful, and they had the type of success I wanted.

I knew intuitively that I had been "assigned" to these women— to learn from them and to follow in their footsteps.

I listened to their instruction and I heeded it.

I benefited from their instruction.

Ruth benefited from Naomi's instruction too. As Ruth walked out in obedience the things that Naomi told her to do, Ruth came to know that the God who brought her *out* of Moab was the God who brought her *to* Boaz.

The same God who sees your ongoing work and productivity, your obsession with doing good, and your ongoing willingness to honor those in authority over you as you follow their instructions is the God who already sees and has prepared a reward for you.

The God who has prepared a blessing for you is the God who is preparing you for the blessing.

ENTERING GOD'S FULL PLAN AND PURPOSE FOR YOUR LIFE

What was God's plan and purpose for Ruth? Her destiny included becoming the wife of Boaz and the mother of a baby named Obed. Obed was the great-grandfather of David, an ancestor of Jesus. Ruth's destiny was to be in the bloodline of our Savior and Lord!

Every time God desires to change a nation, he sends a person who has been changed. That certainly was the case in Ruth's life. God changed her, and she changed history.

You have the capability of ushering a new season into the world. You carry within you the seed of a new season . . . a new revival . . . a new move of God. But to usher in that new season, you must leave the old season.

Ruth—the heathen-born woman from a place that murdered babies—became the ancestor of Jesus, who died to give "born-again" life to the heathen!

Ruth—who was marred, scarred, stained, tainted, distorted, and warped by her early environment—lived out her life in greatness.

What God did in the life of Ruth, He can do in your life.

You must allow God to do His changing and preparation work in you.

You must be willing to disconnect from your past and move toward the presence of greatness in your future.

You must come to the place in your life where you look yourself in the mirror and say:

I am not a product of my past.

I am not a product of my environment.

I am not who other people say that I am.

I am who God says I am.

I am who God is calling me to be.

I am willing to move into the destiny God has prepared for me and that He is preparing me to fulfill.

Do you have the attitude that a person with your background can't succeed?

Deal with it!

God says you can succeed. He says you can have a future that is blessed and fulfilling and eternally rewarding. Ask God today to help you leave your past behind and to embrace all that He has for you.

∽ GOD'S WORD ON LEAH

Leah was the first wife of Jacob, the grandson of Abraham. For much of her married life, Leah lived in the shadow of her beautiful sister, Rachel, who became Jacob's second and more beloved wife. Even though she did not have the love of her husband, Leah had six sons and a daughter: Reuben, Simeon, Levi, Judah, Issachar, Zebulun, and Dinah. The Scripture reference for Leah's story is Genesis 29:15–35, and you will find it in the Appendix to this book.

2

LEAH

"If I could just find Prince Charming to love me . . ."

L eah entered into a marriage with a man who didn't love her. She was the "trick" that a trickster played on a trickster.

To understand how this came to happen to Leah, we need to know something about the other people in her life.

Leah's husband was Jacob. He was Isaac's son, and even before he was born, his personality was revealed. God's Word tells us that Rebekah, Jacob's mother, had a difficult pregnancy. The children "struggled together within her" and when she asked God about it, He said to her, "Two nations are in your womb; two people shall be separated from your body" (Gen. 25:22–23).

At the time Rebekah's twin boys were born, Esau was born first, but Jacob's hand was clutching his heel when he came out of the womb. He was named Jacob, which means "supplanter," or one who lays claim to a position that isn't his. In grabbing hold of Esau's heel, Jacob came out of the womb almost as an extension of Esau—even as a baby, he was laying claim to being the "firstborn," with all the rights and privileges that went with that position.

Jacob was a con man for most of his life. He was a "mama's boy," hanging around the house and enjoying the soft and finer things of life. He learned the manipulative tricks of womanhood—and how to pull a fast one without getting caught. He is described as a "mild man" (Gen. 25:27). Rebekah loved Jacob more than Esau.

Esau, on the other hand, was a skillful hunter and a man of the field. He was hairy and masculine. Isaac loved Esau more than Jacob.

Through the years, and with the help of his conniving mother, Jacob not only tricked Esau out of Esau's birthright, but he also tricked his father, Isaac, into giving him the blessing that was the right of a firstborn son.

Jacob didn't need to do all this. Even before Jacob was born, God had told Rebekah about her twin boys, "the older shall serve the younger" (Gen. 25:23). Jacob was destined to be the ruler. But Jacob became impatient.

Oh, what danger there is in becoming impatient with God's timing! Many times, God promises us things and rather than wait until He gives those things to us, we become anxious and attempt to *make* things happen. We try to manipulate people and situations, but in the end, all we create is a mess. God knows the precise timing for the fulfillment of the things He has promised us and prepared as our destiny. Nothing can stand in the way of His bringing to pass what He wills. God's Word tells us that those who inherit God's promises do so "through faith and patience" (Heb. 6:12).

Circumstances cannot deter what God promises . . . and a change of circumstances cannot bring about His promise.

The economic situation cannot deter what God promises . . . and a change in a person's personal economic situation cannot bring about His promise.

The political scene cannot deter what God promises . . . and a change in political leadership cannot bring about His promise.

Marriage or changes in relationships cannot deter what God promises . . . and a change in relationships cannot bring about His promise.

God is faithful to fulfill His promises, in His timing, by His methods (see 1 Corinthians 1:9).

But Jacob became anxious and took matters into his own hands and rushed ahead into making his destiny come to pass. It didn't work. All he did was put himself in jeopardy of his brother's anger and his father's great disappointment and displeasure.

Fearing for his life and with instructions to marry a woman from his own people, Jacob left his home and went to his uncle Laban's home far to the east of where Isaac, Rebekah, and Esau lived. There Jacob fell in love with Rachel, Laban's younger daughter, whom the Bible describes as being "beautiful of form and appearance." In other words, she was a good-looking woman with a good figure. This phrase "beautiful of form" in Hebrew also means that she was lively, vivacious, and extremely attractive— winsome, alluring, desirable. Jacob agreed to work seven years for Rachel, and because he was so in love with her, the time "seemed only a few days to him" (see Genesis 29:17–20). He was totally smitten by the love bug!

When the time came for Jacob to take Rachel as his bride, Laban prepared a feast for all the men, which no doubt included strong drink. And on the wedding night, Laban, a master con man, deceived the con man Jacob. Laban took his daughter Leah to the bridal chamber to wait for Jacob there.

A LIFE IN THE SHADOWS, A VICTIM IN THE MAKING

Leah was the older sister. The Bible describes her as having "delicate" eyes, or "weak" eyes. She may have been handicapped in her sight, or she may have been cross-eyed, or she may have been timid and weak, with such poor self-esteem that she couldn't look another person in the eyes. Whatever the case, she was *not* desirable to Jacob. She was not "beautiful of form and appearance." She was "inferior" in some way in personality and attractiveness, at least as far as Jacob was concerned.

Now, a woman who lives in the shadow of a stunningly beautiful and vivacious sister *knows* she is in the shadow. She knows she's
not the one who is chosen. She knows she's not favored. She knows
she's "second best." From the time Rachel was born, Leah probably
began to withdraw into herself. But suddenly, her father was taking
her to be Jacob's bride. Can you imagine the conflicting emotions
she must have felt?

You may be wondering how Jacob could have been tricked in this
way. Why didn't he see that it was Leah?

The custom was that a bride was taken covered and fully veiled
into a darkened bridal chamber. The bride did not take the veil from
her face until the next morning. The removal of the veil was a sign
that the marriage was consummated.

So there was Leah. All night she listened to Jacob whispering
sweet nothings into her ear. He spoke to her as if she were the love
of his life. He made love to her, and he also had sex with her. There's
a difference and every woman knows it. Making "love" to someone
is not the same as having sex with someone. Jacob was making love
to Leah that night, thinking that she was Rachel. The next morning,
Leah awoke to greet the man who was now her husband, and he was
gone. He had gone to confront Laban.

God's Word tells us, "Do not be deceived, God is not mocked;
for whatever a man sows, that he will also reap" (Gal. 6:7). Jacob had
sown deception all his life, and he now reaped deception. He was a
trickster, but now he was the one who had been tricked. Laban managed to get Jacob to work seven more years so that he could also have
Rachel as his wife.

For her part, Leah was caught in the manipulation and deception
of two master tricksters. The trick was not of her design.

Have you ever been caught up in someone else's circus?

Have you ever been the person caught in a web of deception that
was not of your creation?

Leah was a victim. And all she ever wanted was what all women want—to be loved. Leah wanted to be loved, admired, and respected for who *she* was.

Isn't that what we all really want in life?

We want our parents to love, admire, and respect us.

We want our spouses, our pastors, our children, our friends to love, admire, and respect us. We want someone in our lives who will affirm us and love us unconditionally. That's what Leah wanted . . . but it is not what Leah got.

When Leah awoke the next morning desiring to be held and loved by her husband, she faced an empty bed. She was alone, rejected, and no doubt felt that she had been used and abandoned, and that she was unwanted and undesirable.

Can you imagine how bad she felt?

Do you know what it feels like to be the "booby prize"?

Being the booby prize might not be so bad if you don't know you're the booby prize, but Leah *knew* she was not the one Jacob wanted.

On that morning, Leah also began her efforts to win Jacob's love and affections. That's what we women do. Leah was in a relationship, and she was determined to do what she could to win the heart of her husband who did not desire her.

A CAMPAIGN TO WIN FAVOR

To what extremes have you gone to win someone's favor? To what lengths have you gone to be the favorite sibling, the only woman in your husband's life, or the person who gets the desired position? We women often do crazy things to get someone's attention and win someone's favor. Why? Because women are relational by nature. God made women that way. If you ask a woman who she is, she'll tell you that she's the wife, mother, daughter, or friend of someone. If you ask a man who he is, he'll tell you about his job or his career title. Men were birthed into productivity and position.

When a person seeks another person's favor, the first step is to get that person's attention. Don't tell me that you've never done something to get a man's attention!

See Me! We live in a world of people who are craving attention. Every person desires attention, and we all do what we think will make us more accepted, important, or needed. We all desire to be listened to . . . to be hugged . . . to be called a person of worth . . . to "belong." When we don't get those emotional strokes, we resort to extreme attention getters. That's what spiked green hair and body piercings and tattoos are all about! People are wanting somebody . . . *anybody* . . . to say, "I see you! I am paying attention to you!"

Many marriages today are suffering from a lack of attention—no kind words, no hugs, no flowers, no words of praise, no home-cooked meals. Attention and affection are closely linked. You can't be affectionate with someone you don't "see" or recognize. And the need for affection and attention moves both ways. Wives need attention and affection from their husbands. Husbands need attention and affection from their wives. Every person who is married sends an SOS on occasion that cries, "Please, at least let me know that you know I'm in the house! Please let me know that you think I'm more important than the television set, the radio, the computer, or the telephone. Please *see me.*"

Leah began a personal campaign to win Jacob's attention and affection, and she pursued the only means available to her—she had a baby. Jacob may not have loved Leah, but he was married to her and it was Leah's "right" in that society at that time to have sex with her husband and to have the opportunity for bearing children. Jacob fulfilled his conjugal duties to her and Leah became pregnant.

Leah named her firstborn son Reuben. His name means "look

at me." Leah thought by giving Jacob a son that Jacob would finally *see* her. She was hoping he would begin to love her. God's Word tells us that she said, "The LORD has surely looked on my affliction. Now therefore, my husband will love me" (Gen. 29:32).

But he didn't.

Leah was married to a man who probably walked into the house at the end of the day and didn't even say hello. He probably had a way of looking at her, but not seeing her. He probably didn't notice if she gained weight or lost weight, was wearing a new dress, or had changed her hairstyle. She was just "there," and even a baby boy didn't cause Jacob to "see" Leah, much less love her.

Something happens to a woman's spirit when she is totally ignored by a man with whom she desires to have a loving relationship. Her psyche is messed up; her heart is crushed; her self-esteem is shattered. Rejection can create deep emotional wounds in any person. After a while, the person begins to say, "Maybe there's something wrong with me. Maybe I'm not what I should be. Maybe I need to try something else to show how valuable I am."

Hear Me! Leah tried a second time. She got pregnant again and had a second son. This son she named Simeon, which means "to hear." In naming her son, Leah was crying out to Jacob, "Listen to me!" She was crying out to have her opinions, her feelings, her desires heard.

One of the worst things any woman can experience is to live with a man who *looks* as if he's hearing and *acts* as if he's listening, but in actuality, he isn't taking in a word that's being said to him. There are so many marriages in which the wife is doing all the talking and the husband is doing all the ignoring. And that, too, does something to a woman's personality and mind. It damages her feelings of self-worth. Every time Leah spoke Simeon's name, she was sending a message to Jacob: "Listen to me."

But he didn't.

Know Me! Leah persisted. She was determined to win Jacob's attention and affection. She had a third son, and this one she named Levi, which means "to be joined to" or "to be connected with." Leah was crying out to Jacob, "Join with me! Connect with me! I'm the one who is giving you sons and making you a father. Rachel isn't bearing fruit from your relationship with her. I'm the one bearing fruit! Can't you see that God is honoring *our* relationship? Can't you see that *our* relationship is the one God is blessing?"

Leah's desire was that Jacob might truly be intimate with her—not just have sex with her, but love her, share his life secrets with her, talk to her in an intimate, sharing, caring way. God's admonition at the time He created Eve from Adam's rib was this: "Therefore a man shall leave his father and mother and be joined to his wife, and they shall become one flesh" (Gen. 2:24). That's the relationship Leah was desperate to experience. Even though she had three children by Jacob, she felt separated from him. She didn't *feel* as if he had ever really joined with her and "become one" with her.

So many people today have been in ceremonies in which rings were exchanged and a marriage license was filed, but no real marriage took place. A ring and a piece of paper don't make a marriage! You can live in the same house and share the same bed with someone, and not have the intimacy and commitment that constitute a *real* marriage.

You can live in the same house and drive around in the same car and go to some of the same places with a spouse, and not be one flesh.

You can sit in church together with your spouse, and not be one flesh.

You can eat at the same table with a spouse year after year, and not be one flesh.

You can have sex with a spouse, and not be one flesh.

In naming her third son Levi, Leah was calling out to Jacob,

"Join with me! Get into this marriage with me! Be intimate with me and be committed to me!"

But he wasn't.

Having children doesn't guarantee that your spouse will see you, hear you, or be intimate and "one" with you. Leah finally faced up to that fact. She shifted gears.

How do you handle adverse situations in your marriage?

What do you do when you cannot get what you want from your husband?

What do you do when things aren't turning out the way you had longed for them to turn out . . . the way you had worked so hard for them to be . . . the way you had prayed and hoped they might develop?

What do you do when a boss bypasses you and promotes the other person?

What do you do when your father loves your sister more than you, or your mother treats your brother with greater affection than she shows you?

What do you do when everything you've tried has absolutely no influence on the person you love—when no matter what you try, you fail to win his love, respect, or admiration?

You need to learn the lesson of Leah! Leah finally reached the point at which she said to herself, *I can't get his attention. He won't listen to me. He won't be one with me. It's time to change direction.*

Praise God! Leah gave birth to a fourth son and she named him Judah, which means "let Jehovah be praised!"

When you get tired of people ignoring you . . .

When you are fed up with people not wanting you around . . .

Switch gears! It's time for you to say, "I don't have to have *your* attention to make me whole. I don't have to have *your* listening ear in order to feel valued. I don't have to be alone. I can find my fulfillment in Jehovah God. I can give birth to *praise* and in my praise, I will be in the *presence* of God. God will see me . . . God will hear me . . . God will be present with me . . . God will make me whole and fulfill my life. Praise Jehovah!"

When your body is racked with pain and nobody seems to care . . . praise Jehovah.

When there are no dollars to buy food for your babies . . . praise Jehovah.

When you've worked all your life for a company and then are "downsized" out of a job . . . praise Jehovah.

When your entire family and all your friends don't seem to understand your relationship with God and start to distance themselves from you . . . praise Jehovah!

There's tremendous freedom from anxiety and inner emotional turmoil when you turn from seeking the attention of people and focus all your heart, mind, and soul on praising the Lord. The more you praise the Lord, the less concerned you become about whether another person sees you or listens to you. The more you praise the Lord, the less anxious you are about whether somebody wants you around or values you.

Why?

Because when you praise the Lord, you restore your true identity. You begin to see God for who God is—not that we can ever fully know all the infinite facets of an eternal God, but we can know that God is more than anything we will ever become. We see God as being all-powerful, all-wise, all-loving, and eternal. We see Him as our rock among the shifting sands of life. We see Him as the balm of Gilead in the midst of our sickness. We see Him as our provider in the midst of our lack. We see Him as eternal and unchanging in the midst of life that is caught up in busyness and one fad after the next.

The more you see who God is, the more you see who He is *to you.* He's not just the rock . . . He's *your* rock. He's not just the balm of Gilead . . . He's *your* healer. He's not just the Provider . . . He's *your* provider.

And the more you see who God is to you, the more you see how valuable you are to Him! He is your rock because He wants you to be stable and steadfast and protected. He wants you to have all that you need, not only to meet your personal need and the needs of your family, but to live in overflowing abundance so you can help meet the needs of others. He wants you to prosper in spirit, mind, and body because He loves you.

Oh, praise Jehovah!

He is the One who created you to be *somebody,* not a nobody.

He is the One who washed you in His blood and cleansed you and lifted you out of guilt and shame.

He is the One who filled you with His love and with the presence of His Holy Spirit.

He is the One who is closer than your breath and who remains the same, yesterday, today, and forever.

The greatest thing you can do to find fulfillment in life is to praise the Lord!

A Life of Praise. Who did the people of the tribe of Judah become down through the years?

They became the leaders, and first and foremost, the leaders in praise. It was from the tribe of Judah that Jesus was born. God bypassed the normal line of succession and He chose Judah to come to the forefront of Jacob's sons. He exalted and promoted Judah, the one who symbolized praise. The "Lion of the tribe of Judah" (see Revelation 5:5) was the ruler of God's people.

Through the centuries, those who follow in the footsteps of the tribe of Judah are those who become addicted to praise. They are the ones who live their lives solely to worship God, and who have a heart's desire to glorify Him. They praise God at the job and as they drive to and from the job. They praise God in the shower and as they are fixing breakfast and working on the car. They praise God in their minds and in their spirits.

King David was from the tribe of Judah (see Matthew 1:2–6). When David accompanied the ark of God into Jerusalem, God's Word tells us that "David danced before the LORD with all his might." He brought up the ark with shouting and with the sound of the trumpet and with gladness. He leaped and whirled before the Lord (see 2 Samuel 6:12–16).

Until you truly become like the tribe of Judah, you will always need people to fulfill you, to "see you," and to "hear you" . . . people to tell you who you are. Once you become a person totally devoted to praise, you will experience the fulfillment of God in your life. You will look to Him and to Him alone to tell you who you are. You will know that you are *somebody.*

You can't praise God and worry about a promotion at the same time.

You can't praise God and be anxious over what another person thinks of you at the same time.

You can't praise God and be frustrated about a relationship at the same time.

Leah birthed Judah and she said, "Now I will praise the Lord!" God's Word tells us "she stopped bearing." She stopped striving to get Jacob's attention. She stopped striving to make things happen in her marriage. Leah found her fulfillment in praise.

MAKING THE CHOICE TO ACCEPT AND EXPERIENCE GOD'S LOVE

Praise brings us face-to-face with the truth of God's love for us. The more you praise God for who He is, the more you are confronted by

His infinite and unchanging care, provision, and protection. In praise, you come to recognize more clearly God's righteousness, holiness, mercy, forgiveness, and grace. In praise, you come to know His love.

Praise brings you to a position in which you must make a decision, and decisions determine destiny. One of the most important decisions you will ever make is the decision to accept God's love for you. God does not force you to love Him. He extends His love to you and invites you to *receive* His love and *experience* His love. You must choose to accept Him.

No person can experience fulfillment until he knows the love of God. The Word of God says:

> For this reason I bow my knees to the Father of our Lord Jesus Christ, from whom the whole family in heaven and earth is named, that He would grant you, according to the riches of His glory, to be strengthened with might through His Spirit in the inner man, that Christ may dwell in your hearts through faith; that you, being rooted and grounded in love, may be able to comprehend with all the saints what is the width and length and depth and height—to know the love of Christ which passes knowledge; that you may be filled with all the fullness of God." (Eph. 3:14–19)

Now, many people have heard that God loves them. The most famous verse in all the Bible tells us, "For God so loved the world that He gave His only begotten Son, that whoever believes in Him should not perish but have everlasting life" (John 3:16). To know with head knowledge that God loves you is not the same, however, as knowing His love personally and experientially. To know the love of God is to know it in your entire being at a deep and intimate level, not just objectively or superficially in your mind.

How do we enter into an experiential "knowing" of God's love? By entering into the presence of God. And how do we do that? By praising Him and worshipping Him. Praise ushers us into the very presence of God, and the more we praise Him, the more our perception changes. We begin to see our lives as God sees us. We begin to understand God's plan and purpose for our lives.

Until we know this love of God, we can't fully love another person.

How can you give what you don't have? If you are empty of God's love, how can you love yourself or love another person? As we drink in of the Lord—taking in His Word, and delighting in His presence in our praise and worship—we find that the Holy Spirit begins to flow in us and out of us as a *river* of God's love to others.

When we discover God's love, we discover that we are God's workmanship—His "product" created "in Christ Jesus for good works, which God prepared beforehand that we should walk in them" (Eph. 2:10). You were not "created" by your mother and father. You were created by God, who formed and fashioned you long before you were in the womb of your mother. God's Word tells us, "Before I formed you in the womb I knew you; before you were born I sanctified you" (Jer. 1:5).

God chose all the attributes for your life, and He knew where to put you, with whom to put you, and how to place you in time and space so that He might raise you up to be a witness of His love and power to this world.

People who don't know that they are God's workmanship often spend a very long time trying to be something they were not created to be. They try to change their appearance and their talents. They try to bypass their cultures or their ethnicity or their genders. God made you, and He made you "fearfully and wonderfully" (Ps. 139:14).

"Wonderfully" means that we are unique. We are one of a kind. It is your uniqueness, your differentness, that makes you special and distinctive.

Nobody can do precisely what you can do.

Nobody can praise like you can praise.

Nobody can love like you can love.

In accepting and experiencing God's love, you discover your own ability to love. You begin to see yourself in a completely different light—you begin to be aware and to say, "I am lovable and I am loving!"

When you catch a glimpse of the future God has for you, you have more hope. You have an understanding: "I'm looking a whole lot better in my future than I'm looking right now!" You begin to walk toward that future, and as you walk toward it as a beloved, prosperous, highly favored, and blessed child of God, you move into that future and it becomes a reality for you.

When we receive God's love, we are then able to pour out His love into the people He brings into our lives. Jesus taught, "You shall love your neighbor as yourself" (Matt. 22:39).

If you are to be the spouse God has destined you to be . . .

Or the parent God has destined you to be to your children . . .

Or the child God has destined you to be to your parents . . .

Or the pastor or minister or leader or friend God has destined you to be . . .

You must have love to give.

A Willingness to Risk Love. How you relate to others around you impacts how you relate to God.

When I was five years old, my father committed suicide. In the next several years after that, I was physically and sexually abused. When I read in my Bible that God desires for us to call Him, "Abba, Father"—which means "Daddy God"—can you imagine how difficult that was for me? How could I crawl up in the lap of Daddy God and trust Him when the only earthly father I had ever known had abandoned and rejected me by killing himself? How could I allow myself to be vulnerable enough to love Daddy God when boys and men I had known had hurt me physically and caused me deep emotional pain?

If you haven't known loving relationships with people, it is even more important that you stay in the presence of God—that your life becomes a life of praise and worship so that you can begin to open yourself up to receiving all that God has for you, including His infinite, unconditional, and tender love. It is in God's presence that your perspective toward His love changes. It is in God's presence that you desire and take the risk of *receiving* God's love.

It is in God's presence that you begin to understand all that God has placed inside you . . . all that He desires to give to you . . . all that He declares is yours as His beloved child and heir. It is in God's presence that you begin to see your problem as "no problem" because God is your loving Father, who will provide for you and protect you.

It is in God's presence that you are empowered to love yourself— to accept yourself as the beloved child God has made, to believe in God's purpose for you, to acknowledge the gifts He has imparted to you, and to have the courage to step out in the ministry He has destined for you.

Whatever God calls you to begin, He will be faithful to sustain.

The meaning of this passage is echoed in 2 Timothy 1:12: "Nevertheless I am not ashamed: for I know whom I have believed and I am persuaded that He is able to keep that which I have committed to Him against that day." God does not call us to failure. He calls us to fulfillment. He calls us to succeed at the things to which He directs us to put our hands and our hearts.

The God who saved you will sustain your salvation until it is brought to fulfillment in eternity.

The God who brought you out of poverty will sustain you out of poverty until your purpose on this earth is fulfilled.

The God who gave you children will sustain you in raising those children and being a parent to them all the rest of your life.

The God who calls you to begin a ministry will sustain you in that ministry until the purpose for your ministry is fulfilled.

Whatever God begins in you, He continues to do in you.

On a foundation of God's loving presence and God's peace, you will be empowered to walk away from those relationships in your life that are toxic—poisonous, damaging, even deadly.

WALKING AWAY FROM TOXIC RELATIONSHIPS

When God wants to bless you, how does He do it? He sends people into your life. When the devil wants to destroy you, how does He do it? He sends people!

There are several types of relationships that are liabilities, not assets. If you are going to develop healthy relationships, you first must cut off the unhealthy ones you have developed.

How can you tell if a relationship is toxic? Here are three major indicators:

- *Constant Strife and Division.* First, there will be constant strife and division. Amos 3:3 asks us, "Can two walk together, unless they are agreed?" A healthy relationship is one in which there is a oneness of goals, purpose, values, and beliefs. God's Word also says, "Where envy and self-seeking exist, confusion and every evil thing are there" (James 3:16).

The Greek word for *confusion* means "unstable." The Bible tells us that a double-minded man is "unstable in all his ways" (James 1:8). The situation is out of order and therefore out of control. God is a God of order. He has set up lines of authority, and when those lines are violated, the door is open to every type of evil spirit. You don't get to choose the brand of evil spirit you want. When you get out of line with the way God has designed things to work, the devil has a legal right to touch you with any form of evil he wants.

Strife and confusion sap your energy and drain your creativity. They take your focus off what God has for you.

- *People Who Knew You "Back When."* One of the most dangerous relationships is the one that holds you to your past. The Bible tells us that when Jesus went to his "own country," He taught, and the people were astonished, but they were also "offended" at Him because they kept saying, "Isn't this the carpenter's son? Isn't this the son of Mary and the brother of James, Joses, Simon, and Judas? He can't possibly have all this wisdom and do these mighty works. We know Him. He's just one of us." And Jesus could do no miracles there "because of their unbelief." It wasn't that Jesus had lost any power in Himself. He wasn't any less of who He was in his home country. It was because of *their* unbelief that He could not manifest the fullness of Himself (see Matthew 13:53–58).

The associations of your past can drag you down and hold you back. They can keep you from fulfilling your potential.

I'm not talking, of course, of relationships that you have entered into with a covenant or relationships that God has ordained for your life. You can't just casually walk away from a father or mother or spouse or child. I'm talking about friendships and business associations and casual acquaintances and distant relatives who remind you continually of what people *used* to think of you. Those old opinions that were not God's opinions are opinions that do not relate to your tomorrow. They relate only to your yesterday.

- *Violators of the Heart.* These are relationships that prey on your heart and rob you of control over your life. Don't give power to *any* person to manipulate you and control you. Nobody deserves that power but God! No person can make you lose your joy, your mind, your temper, or any other aspect unless you *give* that person the power. Don't do it!

The most dangerous violator of the heart is the person who tells you what you want to hear. It is the person who strokes your ego and tells you words of affection that you are desperate to hear, all in an effort to get what *they* want from you.

Violators take advantage of the "needs" in your life, especially the needs to be loved and accepted. They aren't concerned about *your* blessings or *your* destiny. They are concerned only about what they want. They are takers, not givers.

Never lose your identity for another person's sake.

Never compromise your character for anyone.

You must continually take inventory of whether a person is drawing more from you than the person is giving to you. A healthy relationship is a relationship in which there is balance in giving and taking . . . where there is mutual appreciation and a building up . . . where there are honest words of appreciation without any taint of manipulation.

THE STEPS TO CUTTING OFF AN UNHEALTHY RELATIONSHIP

So what are the steps you must take to cut unhealthy relationships out of your life?

First, you must identify and accept the reality of an out-of-balance relationship. At times, you need to take stock of the situation and admit to yourself that a relationship just isn't working. All of your efforts at helping or rehabilitating a person have failed. It is at that point that you need to give that person over to God. Notice that I didn't say that you give up on the person. To give up is to walk away and say, "I don't care what happens to you." To give a person "over to God" is to walk away as you say, "I have done all that I can do. I'm entrusting you to God from this point on."

When you give a person over to Almighty God, you are releasing that person from your own heart to One who truly can heal the person, who will never fail the person, and who is totally qualified to counsel and guide and help the person. How many times can you tell a person the same things over and over and over again? Some people have been prayed for with the laying on of your hands so often that your handprints are indelibly printed on them!

If you allow yourself to be drained and distracted by someone you truly cannot help because that person does not truly *want* your help—only your association—then you will not be in position to help those who truly want your help more than they want your association.

Second, don't try to be God to another person. There's a huge difference between helping a person and carrying a person. You aren't the Holy Spirit. Don't enter into an enabling relationship in which you come to feel totally responsible for a person's success or failure.

Third, become comfortable with criticism. If you do have to end a relationship, not everybody is going to be happy with your decision. For that matter, not everybody is going to be happy with you at *any point* or regarding *anything!* There's always going to be somebody who wants you to do something other than what God is leading you to do. Nobody can please all people all the time, everywhere.

Luke 6:26 tells us, "Woe to you when all men speak well of you, for so did their fathers to the false prophets." Occasionally you need to recognize that hurting people sometimes *hurt* people, and you need to be brave enough and godly enough to say, "This relationship isn't helping you or me. This relationship isn't healthy. We need to put an end to this."

Trust God to help you recognize when a relationship is becoming detrimental to your business, your ministry, or the health of your family life. Trust God to give you the courage to end the relationship, and then trust Him to give you broad enough shoulders and thick enough skin to take the criticism that you may face for ending the relationship.

Fourth, progressively end unhealthy relationships. It takes emotional energy to end a relationship, and if you cut every unhealthy relationship out of your life at one time, you are likely to be overwhelmed by the loss. Cut unhealthy relationships out of your life one at a time until you can look around you and say, "All of my relationships are ones that are pleasing to God. All of my relationships are ones in which there is a mutual give-and-take, a mutual blessing, a mutual edification. I am on the same wavelength with those who are close to me when it comes to values, beliefs, and goals."

Fifth, don't burn bridges. When you dissolve a relationship, don't do so in anger or bitterness. There is a way to walk away from a relationship without words of hatred or criticism or the placing of blame. At the same time, walk away from an unhealthy relationship with the full intent that you will not revisit that relationship in the future. God may lead you to have a relationship with that person down the line, but *you* should not have the intent to come back to the relationship. Make a clean break. Make a definitive break.

There may be a situation in which someone comes to you to break off a relationship. Allow that break to occur. Don't keep hanging on. Don't keep trying to mend fences that are twelve-foot-high stone walls. Don't keep revisiting the relationship in your heart, looking for a way back in. Allow the break to happen.

And then, move forward. If you continue to look back, you

won't be qualified or given the authority to possess what God has for you. Look ahead, not back.

Every time you look back, you begin to question, "Did I do the right thing?" You second-guess your today. You become hesitant about your tomorrow. Leave the past behind. Move forward!

When my husband, Randy, and I left Washington, D.C., for Tampa, Florida, we had a word from God and we knew that God had called us, but we didn't know that twelve years later, there would be fifteen thousand people who would call themselves members of Without Walls Church. We didn't know there would be twenty thousand people who would receive help from more than 240 outreach ministries on a weekly basis.

On the way to Tampa, we were in South Carolina with a little U-Haul trailer filled with a few little sentimental items, and we broke down. I started thinking, *Have we lost our minds? Have we made the biggest mistake of our lives?* A little straggling dog came up to our car by the side of the road, and I began to feed it a few scraps of bread. My husband, Randy, said to me, "You'd better not give all your bread to that dog. It might be the only food you have for the next two weeks." He meant it!

Don't look at what might have been, should have been, or could have been! Look at what is still to be!

Go to Those Who Celebrate You. Why waste your life trying to get the attention or win the affection of people who don't care about you?

Why make the effort to go where people merely tolerate you but don't celebrate you?

Why spend your time, effort, and resources seeking acceptance from people who are so wrapped up in themselves that they can't accommodate anybody else in their lives?

Why spend your spiritual gifts on people who aren't at all capable of recognizing and appreciating the One who lives inside you?

Jesus told a parable in which a man gave a great feast and invited many people to come. He sent his servant at the appointed time to say to those who were invited, "Come, for all things are now ready." But one by one, those who were invited made excuses. One had bought some property, another a new yoke of oxen he needed to "test," and another had just married.

Aren't those the things that people tend to value more than *you* today? One person has a business that he values more than you, another a new car or new boat or some other new "toy" of some value that the person needs to "test out." Another has a new relationship that is more important than the relationship with you.

Find the people who are starving for what *you* offer! Find people who want who you are, what you give, and what you celebrate.

THE FOUNDATION FOR GOOD RELATIONSHIPS

How do we develop healthy relationships? It is important that you form partnerships and associations based upon a common direction and the same destination.

- *A Common Direction.* You must be in relationship with people who have a common direction—common values and goals. If you do not have a common direction, you will be in conflict continually.

The most important question to ask in any relationship is, "Are you going my way?"

God's blessing is on unity among His people. God's Word says, "Keep the unity of the Spirit in the bond of peace. There is one body and one Spirit, just as you were called in one hope of your calling; one Lord, one faith, one baptism; one God and Father of all, who is above all, and through all, and in you all" (Eph. 4:3–4).

Marriages, families, ministries, businesses, churches, and friendships all need unity. They need to be based on the things that make us "one."

To come into unity means to come into agreement. Agreement means "to pursue a conscious decision to work together and meet by appointment." You must make a decision to walk in agreement with another person. You must make a decision to meet together with regularity to renew your agreement. In our ministry and church, every staff member is challenged to come into agreement and stay in agreement with our vision for evangelism and restoration. In a marriage, if one spouse wants to live in the south part of the city and the other spouse wants to live in the north, there will be conflict. No agreement means no unity. No unity means no blessing.

Unity takes effort. The apostle Paul wrote to the Ephesians that in order to walk in unity and to walk worthy of the calling with which they were called, they had to have all "lowliness and gentleness, with long-suffering, bearing with one another in love, endeavoring to keep the unity of the Spirit in the bond of peace" (Eph. 4:1–3). *Lowliness* means humility. *Long-suffering* means patience. *Bearing* and *endeavoring* are words related to working. It goes against our nature to be humble. It goes against our culture to be patient. It goes against human nature to be "gentle and loving" with people who are different from us. It goes against our pride to "bear with" other people in love and to endeavor to keep peace. But without unity and agreement, there is no blessing.

- *The Same Destination.* To have the same destination is to have a conscious commitment to a common goal.

When I met my Randy, he was much heavier than he is today. He had a bowl haircut, and he wore green-velvet bow ties and platform shoes and polyester suits. He had no money.

I did not marry my husband for his looks, his fashion sense, or his wealth. The important point is that all of those things could be changed without changing who Randy was on the inside. I knew a great barber, a good tailor, and an effective diet plan. What I never wanted to change, and knew I could not change, was the man Randy is on the inside. That is the authentic person. The genuine person is not the outside package, but the treasure, gifting, and values that are within. Many people falsely market themselves—especially while dating. They sell themselves as beautiful, quiet, meek, and laid back. Then two years into the marriage they have an "in your face" attitude. You need to know a person before you enter into covenant with them. How do they treat people who they don't need in their lives? Where are they heading? What is their destination? What do they value?

So many women meet men who are handsome and seem to have it all together in their appearances and careers—they drive the big cars and have the flashy clothes and the polished looks—and they marry those men before they truly know them. They end up falling for the exterior packaging and don't pay enough attention to the gift inside. They spend years, decades, even their lifetimes trying to change the man on the inside. And you cannot change a person—only God can change the nature of a person. Jeremiah 13:23 reminds us: "Can an Ethiopian change his skin, or the leopard his spots? Then may ye also do good, that are accustomed to evil."

What a woman needs to do is to find a man who has the character and qualities she wants on the *inside* and make certain that he's moving toward the same goals in life that she has. The outside appearance is what can be changed, if necessary, as the months and years go by.

I married Randy because the more we got to know each other, the more we came to an understanding that we wanted to end up at the same place in life. I wasn't sure how we'd get there, but I knew we had the same goals and the same destination. We had a common direction, but the most important thing was that we had the same destination in mind. Our destination was identifiable. It was something we talked about. It was something we could focus on. It was something we both recognized and acknowledged as being very important.

God tells us very clearly that He has a *deliberate destination* for us as His children. Jeremiah 29:11 declares: "For I know the thoughts that I think toward you," saith the Lord, "thoughts of peace, and not of evil, to give you an expected end." God says His thoughts toward us are for peace, which in Hebrew is *Shalom*. It literally means thoughts of safety, wellness, happiness, great health, prosperity, favor, rest, and completeness. In other words, "nothing missing and nothing broken" from your life. God has an expected end for you.

Are the people you choose to have in your life going your same direction toward your same destination? Are you helping others—and are they helping you—to "come to the unity of the faith and of the knowledge of the Son of God?"

ONLY GOD CAN COMPLETE YOU

Are you struggling today with the fact that someone you love doesn't love you? Are you feeling rejected? Are you waiting for someone to come along to "complete" you with his love?

Deal with it!

Recognize that no other human being can ever complete you. Only God can do that work. Make the choice to accept and experience His love. Open your mouth to praise Him for His love. Grow in His love. And then begin to give His love.

If you need to cut away toxic relationships from your life, ask the Lord to give you the courage to do that. If you need to build stronger, healthier relationships, ask the Lord to help you establish those relationships on a firm foundation. If you need to mend a torn relationship, ask the Lord to heal the relationship and to help you become a loving agent of His healing power.

Find your place in the love of God, and you'll find your place in the hearts of those God puts in your life.

⌒ GOD'S WORD ON RAHAB

Rahab lived in Jericho, where she gave shelter to two Israelite spies at the time Joshua and the Israelites entered the promised land. Believing that Jericho would fall to the Israelites, Rahab took the initiative in declaring her faith in God and arranging for the deliverance of her entire family. God honored her faith and courage by allowing her to escape destruction, marry an Israelite, and to be one of the ancestors of Jesus. The Scripture reference for Rahab's story is Joshua 2:12–20, and you will find it in the Appendix to this book.

3

RAHAB

"What do you mean, I have to change my life?"

Rahab was a woman who was living in a city that was on the verge of conquest—and she intuitively knew it. She was a woman looking into a future in which destruction seemed inevitable. Her situation, from a human perspective, was utterly helpless and hopeless.

Have you ever felt you were on the brink of destruction?

Does it seem as if there's "no way out" of a devastating situation you are in?

Do you know what it feels like to look into the future and see *nothing?*

Have you ever walked through a situation that you never thought you'd have to walk through? Are you walking through that situation today?

When you are in a crisis that seems hopeless and helpless, life can become filled with confusion. Confusion means disorder, disturbance, commotion, tumult. It is the opposite of peace. We know from God's Word that confusion is *not* from God. The Bible says, "God is not the author of confusion but of peace, as in all the churches of the saints" (1 Cor. 14:33).

Nonetheless, confusion can strike anyone. Even a righteous saint can face a situation that seems helpless, hopeless, and filled with confusion. God's Word tells us that Job, the most righteous man on the earth in his day, declared, "If I am wicked, woe to me; even if I am righteous, I cannot lift up my head. I am full of disgrace; see my misery!" (Job 10:15).

So what are we to conclude about a crisis and confusion? We must conclude that God can *use* a crisis and a time of confusion in our lives to bring us to a decision that will result in a blessing.

A crisis is a situation in which your future will take one direction or the other—it will get better, or get worse. A crisis has embedded within it an opportunity—the opportunity to make a good decision that will produce a good result. In Rahab's case, it would have been difficult to imagine a way out of the confusion, out of the crisis, out of devastation. It would have been difficult to imagine any decision she could make that would result in her blessing. But . . . God is a God who creates a way where there seems to be no way.

Rabah was not a cute little Sunday-school girl. She was a Canaanite whore, but she was not a cheap "floozy Suzy" who walked the streets of Jericho. The Canaanites were idolaters who worshipped many gods. She was part of a high-class fertility cult that conducted lewd, immoral acts with so-called "sacred" prostitutes. In all of her mess, she *thought* she was a spiritual person.

How many people fall into that category today? They act like the devil with a blue dress most of the time, but because they go to church a few Sundays a year, they think they're "spiritual." Because they think about God occasionally, or listen to a Christian television program now and then, or toss a dollar or two into an offering plate occasionally, they think they are right with God.

We need to understand that everything that's spiritual isn't Christlike or godly.

We need to understand that there's a huge difference between being "religious" on occasion and having a *relationship* with Jesus Christ.

We also need to understand that there is a high cost to sexual encounters that are apart from God's commandments. It doesn't matter what you do that might fall into the "religious" category. God's Word says, "Whoever commits adultery with a woman lacks understanding; he who does so destroys his own soul" (Prov. 6:32). The apostle Paul wrote to the Corinthians, "Flee sexual immorality. Every sin that a man does is outside the body, but he who commits sexual immorality sins against his own body. Or do you not know that your body is the temple of the Holy Spirit who is in you, whom you have from God, and you are not your own? For you were bought at a price; therefore glorify God in your body and in your spirit, which are God's" (1 Cor. 6:18–20).

The price of sexual sin is destruction against both the soul and the body.

It doesn't matter if you don't know that you are breaking God's commandment. The end result is the same. Sexual sin erodes a person's self-worth even if that person *thinks* he is doing something good or acceptable. Sexual sin erodes a person's sense of value even if the person doesn't know he has committed sexual sin. That's why people who don't have any restraint when it comes to sexual sin find that they feel empty, emotionally bankrupt, and void "the morning after." No matter how good a time you thought you had, you feel bad about yourself later.

We treat vessels—bowls, vases, pitchers, and so forth—based upon our discernment of their value. We freely handle a plastic pitcher that costs us two or three dollars, but we handle with extreme care the ornate porcelain vase that costs two or three thousand dollars. The same is true for the way we handle our physical bodies, which are also vessels. God's Word says, "Abstain from sexual immorality; that each of you should know how to possess his own vessel in sanctification and honor, not in passion of lust" (1 Thess. 4:3–5). Those who freely give themselves sexually to others do so because they do not value their bodies. When you do not value your body, you do not value your entire self.

What is with you, around you, and part of your life gives you your sense of self-worth. You unconsciously attract what you have come to think you deserve. That was the situation in Jericho. We know that as a cult prostitute, Rahab didn't value herself. She was in an environment and culture that had trained her through the years *not* to value herself.

THE OUTSIDE DOESN'T ALWAYS SHOW WHAT'S INSIDE

From casual observance, you would not necessarily have recognized that Rahab didn't value herself very highly. On the outside, Rahab had a lot going for her. She was an extremely beautiful woman. She is one of the few women in the Bible who is described as very beautiful. According to Rabbinic tradition, Rahab was one of the four most beautiful women in the history of the world. She was also a very wealthy woman. She owned her own house—a large home on the wall of the city, which was prime real estate. She may even have had a regional reputation as a businesswoman since Jericho was an important trade-center city and Rahab ran a business of manufacturing and dying linen cloth. She was influential, for we know as we read her story that she had access to the king of the city.

But if you watched Rahab for a while—if you watched the way she walked and talked and carried herself—she would have given indications about the way she felt on the inside. Her *actions* are what would have told you she had low self-esteem. She was a woman who had so much on the outside . . . but had so little on the inside.

She no doubt was physically exhausted as well as emotionally exhausted. Don't tell me that a woman who is running her own business, running a large house, and acting as a fertility-cult prostitute isn't physically exhausted! She may not have looked exhausted—her makeup and hairdo and clothes may have hidden the slump in her shoulders and the slowness of her walk by the end of a day, but she was exhausted nonetheless. She was exhausted by *life*.

Public Success, Private Failure. We see many people in our world today who are public successes and private failures.

In our ministry, Randy and I have had the privilege and responsibility of dealing with a number of high-profile and wealthy people—people who have known a great deal of success and fame as far as the world is concerned. One of these people said to us one time, "I was walking in four-thousand-dollar alligator shoes, but I wasn't going anywhere. I was sleeping in a twenty-thousand-dollar bed, but I wasn't getting any rest. I had luxury cars, but I was contemplating driving one of those cars off a bridge and killing myself."

Especially in the church, we need to allow people to be open and transparent so they can lay down their masks and be real before God and before other people.

The truth is, many of those who call themselves Christians are a mess on the inside! They may put up a wonderful exterior facade, but inside, they are hurting, suffering, and sin-filled.

There's something terribly wrong when Christians divorce at a rate that is higher than the secular world.

There's something terribly wrong when convention planners report that pornography consumption in a city's hotels goes up dramatically when a Christian convention comes into that city.

When we accept Christ, we don't immediately die to all sinful impulses and desires. We must die to the flesh *daily*. We must put off the character of the old man and put on the character of the new man day in and day out (see Ephesians 4:22–24).

Never allow yourself to be fooled by the outer appearance of the person. A person might drive a fancy car and wear designer clothes and look at all times as if she just came from a spa . . . and still have *nothing* on the inside. God's Word tells us that there's only one thing that fills us on the inside: knowing the love of Christ. Knowing refers to an intimate relationship—not just to "know about" something with a head knowledge, but to know from close personal experience. That, according to Ephesians 3:19, is what allows a person to "be filled with all the fullness of God."

Money doesn't fulfill us. It isn't position or fame or beauty or education or a spouse. It isn't even having a ministry. The *only* thing that can fill a person with "fullness" is to know the love of Christ.

You can only overcome your condition when you know your position. As long as you are focusing on the condition of your life—the symptoms, the externals—you will not get to the root of the problem. You must examine yourself within if you are going to overcome your external problems. It is as you examine yourself within that you can begin to discover the greatness that God has deposited in you. You begin to see yourself as a vessel with hidden treasure. God's Word says, "But we have this treasure in earthen vessels, that the excellence of the power may be of God and not of us" (2 Cor. 4:7). The treasure in you is filled with possibilities and potentialities. When you begin to bring forth the treasure that God has put in you, your entire life begins to change.

The enemy of your soul doesn't want you to bring forth the treasure in you. He doesn't want you to give birth to the potentialities and promises of God in you. If you begin to bring forth the hidden treasure inside you, the devil will send distractions to you to make you doubt what you have discovered. The devil sends distractions to disillusion you, depress you, and defeat you. Distractions make you question: "Can I really do what I *thought* God said I could do? Can I really be who I *thought* God said I could be? Can I really have what I *thought* God said I could have?"

Distractions are inevitably linked to some form of battle, struggle, or warfare. Rahab lived in Jericho, a city known for battles and struggles.

When battles come to distract you, you must cling to the truth that God has called you with an *eternal* purpose. No matter where you are right now, it's not where you are going to be. God's Word says, "He who has begun a good work in you will complete it until the day of Jesus Christ" (Phil. 1:6). God has an appointed task for you. He is doing a good work in you. He is the One who is the author of the work in you, and He is the One who will finish it. What you are going through may be a chapter in your life, but it's not the end of the book.

ACKNOWLEDGING GOD AS LORD OF HEAVEN AND EARTH

In the midst of her crisis moment—facing the very real possibility of battle and devastation—Rahab says, "For the LORD your God, He is God in heaven above and on earth beneath" (Josh. 2:11).

So much is being said in just that one statement! Rahab is a harlot, a depleted and spent-out woman, emotionally drained, physically exhausted, empty. And in that state, she says to the two Israelite spies who come to her home, "I know that your God, the Lord, is God in heaven above and earth beneath." In other words, "What men cannot do for me . . . what money cannot do for me . . . what religion cannot do for me . . . your God can do. He is able to do all things. He is God of all the heavens above and all the earth. He has all power and authority to meet *all* the needs in my life."

It is out of Rahab's recognition that God has the ability to do what nothing and no one else could do, that she cries out for the deliverance of herself and her entire family.

There are three things I don't want you to miss:

First, God hears the heart's cry of every person who calls out to Him and declares that He is Lord over heaven and earth. Jesus said, "For God so loved the world . . . that whoever believes in Him . . ." (John 3:16).

Whoever means *whoever!* It doesn't matter if you are man or woman, young or old, educated or uneducated, rich or poor. It doesn't matter your culture or race or nationality.

Second, God does not determine the promise of your future by looking at the condition of your past. It doesn't matter where you have been or what you have done in your miserable messed-up past. All of God's promises are available to you the moment you cry out to Him for deliverance and salvation. Acts 10:34 assures us, "God shows no partiality. But in every nation whoever fears Him and works righteousness is accepted by Him." To "fear" God in that verse is to show awe, respect, and honor to God. It is to recognize that Almighty God is the Lord over the heavens and the earth. To fear God is to acknowledge that His ways are higher than any ways man can create and that His plans are better, more effective, and infinitely more blessed than any plans man can generate.

Third, your faith is what God honors. God does not look at your past mistakes and exclude you from His promises. Neither does God give you His promises on the basis of any good works you have done. It is your *faith* in Him that brings God's promises to you.

God doesn't look at your résumé. He isn't impressed with your cuteness or your cleanness. God says, "If you will give me your faith, I will give you your future." God's Word says, "There is therefore now no condemnation to those who are in Christ Jesus, who do not walk according to the flesh, but according to the Spirit" (Rom. 8:1).

You are raised up solely by the blood of Jesus. It doesn't matter if you've had three abortions, five men, two children out of wedlock, or been on welfare far too long, or if you've been in church all your life and have never lied, cheated, slept around, or even put your hand in the cookie jar and stolen a cookie. God doesn't raise us up because we do good things or don't do good things. He raises us up because we have faith in the finished work of Christ Jesus on the cross. God can take a whore and a virgin and raise them up to the same level if they will trust in Him and put their total assurance in Him. Faith is equal-opportunity business.

If you can *believe* . . . God will rebuild your broken life.

If you can *believe* . . . God will restore your broken home.

If you can *believe* . . . God will remold your broken dreams.

Rahab believed God to save her entire family, even as destruction was on the horizon. When Jericho fell, all of Rahab's household was saved—all her family and all she had (see Joshua 2:13 and 6:25). Houses all around Rahab's fell and families all around Rahab's family were killed, but God saved the whorehouse. He saved all of Rahab's family that was in the house with her. He spared all the material wealth she could carry from the city with her. He saved her because she put her faith in Him as the Lord in heaven above and the earth beneath.

If you believe today that your background is keeping you from moving forward with God, then you don't understand that the only thing God is asking from you is for you to have faith in Him.

If you believe today that God will act on your behalf because He is moved by your faults or failures, then you don't understand that the only thing that moves God is your faith.

God does not save you because He feels sorry for you.

He does not deliver you because you are in a bad place.

He does not bless you because you have great need.

God saves and delivers and blesses because you cry out to Him with your faith.

Faith Must Be Activated. Faith is what empowers you to attain all that the Father has promised to you. But . . . your faith must be *activated*. God's Word says, "Likewise, was not Rahab the harlot also justified by works when she received the messengers and sent them out another way? For as the body without the spirit is dead, so faith without works is dead also" (James 2:25–26). In other words, you must initiate or act upon what God has promised to you.

The Bible also says, "Be doers of the word, and not hearers only, deceiving yourselves" (James 1:22).

What is it that we are to do as we act on our faith? We are to step out on God's Word and obey it. We are to sow seeds. We are to start giving. We are to start helping others. The book of Ephesians says, "Whatever good anyone does, he will receive the same from the Lord, whether he is a slave or free" (6:8). What you make happen for others, God will make happen for you.

When you ask of God . . . ask large.

When you believe for something from God . . . believe large.

Stop waiting for someone to come along and help you out. Passivity will always keep you from receiving what God wants to give you.

Get up, get busy, and start reaching out to others, trusting God—believing in Him, having assurance in Him, having faith in Him—to cause something significant to happen in you!

Rahab *asked* to be saved. She took the initiative. She said, "I beg you, swear to me by the LORD, since I have shown you kindness, that you also will show kindness to my father's house . . . and deliver our lives from death" (Josh. 2:12–13).

A CHOICE TO FOLLOW GOD'S INSTRUCTIONS

Rahab was given very specific instructions by the spies to whom she had given shelter and to whom she offered a way of escape. She listened to these men and followed the instructions they gave her.

Throughout God's Word, we are given instructions. At the end of his life, Moses said to the Israelites, "See, I have set before you today life and good, death and evil, in that I command you today to love the LORD your God, to walk in His ways, and to keep His commandments, His statutes, and His judgments, that you may live and multiply; and the LORD your God will bless you in the land which you go to possess" (Deut. 30:15–16). All of the laws that had been given to Moses were given so that the people of God might "live and multiply." They were laws that set up the people to be blessed in the land that they were to go in and possess.

The same is true for God's commands to us. They are laid out before us as a choice—we can *choose* whether we will obey or disobey. They are laid out to us for our blessing, so that we might live and multiply and possess all God has for us. They are laid out with consequences. If we choose not to obey the instructions God gives us, we face consequences for our rebellion. We may not like those consequences, but we receive them nonetheless. We may not like the way God instructs us or sets up His system of commandments and statutes and judgments, but God has established the system nonetheless.

Rahab had a choice. She *chose* to follow the instructions given to her by the Israelite spies.

Do fixed principles guide your heart and your mind?

Is your "yes" always a yes, and your "no" always a no?

Do you live a life of integrity?

Do you accept God's authority over you and choose to follow His instructions?

The Israelite spies were very clear with Rahab. They were willing to make an agreement with her: "Our lives for yours." But, they also made it very clear that if she did not do precisely what they instructed her to do, they would not be responsible for her certain death. Rahab replied to them, "According to your words, so be it" (Josh. 2:21).

God calls us to obedience. He tells us that He desires our obedience more than sacrifice (see 1 Samuel 15:22). In other words, God wants us to say "yes" to His commandments and instructions so that we won't sin, rather than find ourselves in a situation where we have to request forgiveness for having committed the sin. If you are walking in obedience, you won't *need* to make a sin-offering sacrifice, pleading for forgiveness and restoration!

PUT A SCARLET CORD IN THE WINDOW

The spies said to Rahab, "When we come into the land, you bind this line of scarlet cord in the window through which you let us down" (Josh. 2:18).

The scarlet cord was a type, a symbol, a representative sign that spoke to the Israelites of the blood covenant that God had with His people. On the night that God delivered the Israelites from Egypt, God told the people to put blood on the lintel and side posts of their doors. Moses said to the people, "The LORD will pass through to strike the Egyptians; and when He sees the blood on the lintel and on the two doorposts, the LORD will pass over the door and not allow the destroyer to come into your houses to strike you" (Ex. 12:23). The scarlet cord in Rahab's window was a sign that read loud and clear to the Israelites, "Do not destroy this house."

The scarlet cord means to us today that God sends a similar message to the enemy of our souls when the shed blood of Jesus has been applied to our "temple," which is our life. The devil has no legal right or authority to cross the "bloodline" to kill us for all eternity.

Let me remind you of some things related to the shed blood of Jesus on the cross.

First, His shed blood makes atonement for sin. God's Word says, "For the life of the flesh is in the blood, and I have given it to you upon the altar to make atonement for your souls; for it is the blood that makes atonement for the soul" (Lev. 17:11). Atonement means that we are back in relationship with God. Atonement means that we are reunited with a God after having been separated from Him because of our sin and rebellion. Atonement means that we are forgiven.

Second, His shed blood redeems, cleanses, and purifies. Read what God's Word says about the power of the blood:

- "You were not redeemed with corruptible things, like silver or gold, from your aimless conduct received by tradition from your fathers, but with the precious blood of Christ, as of a lamb without blemish and without spot" (1 Peter 1:18–19). The shed blood of Jesus Christ bought you off the slave market of sin so that the devil no longer has you under his bondage. You have been given the power to say "no" to sin and to the devil, and "yes" to God. You have been given the power to live in the "yes zone"—always and continually saying "yes" to God whenever and whatever and wherever He commands you! It's that redemptive power of the shed blood of Jesus that gives you the power and ability to live in a way that "you may not sin" (1 John 2:1).

- "How much more shall the blood of Christ, who through the eternal Spirit offered Himself without spot to God, cleanse your conscience from dead works to serve the living God?" (Heb. 9:14). The blood of Christ creates in us a new awareness and understanding of what is right and wrong. It changes our priorities, our perspectives, our passions, and our pursuits. Because of what Jesus did for us, we no longer strive to serve those things that are temporary and fruitless, but rather, those things that are eternal and fruitful!

- "To Him who loved us and washed us from our sins in His own blood, and has made us kings and priests to His God and Father, to Him be glory and dominion forever and ever" (Rev. 1:5–6). God cleanses us from our sins—He washes them away from our memories, from having any influence over us, from having any bearing or consequence on our eternal reward. His cleansing is so complete that we are qualified to be kings and priests of His kingdom on this earth. His cleansing qualifies us for leadership, for holiness, for service.

Get a new vision for what the shed blood of Jesus means to *you!* It is because He died for you that you can *live*—not only an abundant life now, but an eternal life . . . not only a righteous life now, but a glorious life forever . . . not only a purified past, but a rewarding and blessed and fulfilling life throughout the endless ages to come.

Binding the Cord of Your Salvation. Rahab "bound the scarlet cord in the window" (Josh. 2:21). To *bind* is to attach, to fix, to tie in a way that cannot be untied.

That's what we are called to do. We are to bind ourselves to Christ Jesus in a way that nobody and no circumstance and no experience and no event and no force can "undo" us. We are to refuse any temptation that would cause us to become less committed or less obedient.

You know the temptations I'm talking about. You're probably thinking of one right now.

You know the temptation to sleep in and miss church "just this once."

You know the temptation to buy that item you really want rather than give your tithe this month.

You know the temptation to stall in volunteering to help with that ministry because you'd rather spend time doing something else.

You know the temptation that tells you to read your Bible twice as much tomorrow and never mind reading it today because today is a very busy day.

You know the temptation that comes to skip your prayer time with the Lord because you probably have already done enough praising for one week.

There are countless temptations that come at us to get us to be just a little less obedient, just a little less committed. The enemy doesn't come with a temptation to deny Christ or to renounce God. The enemy comes with a temptation to move away from a close, intimate "knowing" of God just a little bit here, a little bit there, one decision, one commitment, and one choice at a time.

STAY IN THE HOUSE

Rahab received a second instruction from the spies: Stay in the house. The spies said, "So it shall be that whoever goes outside the doors of your house into the street, his blood shall be on his own head, and we will be guiltless. And whoever is with you in the house, his blood shall be on our head if a hand is laid on him" (Josh. 2:19).

Stay in the covenant of God.

Stay steadfast in your faith.

Stay in your place of assignment that God has given you.

Stay in the place that God has provided for your spiritual covering.

You may not understand why God hasn't worked yet on your behalf. You may be puzzled as to why God hasn't caused you to have a breakthrough. You may be wondering why God hasn't provided for you in the way you believe He will . . . but don't allow your lack of understanding to cause you to move out from under the umbrella of your protection.

Don't allow yourself to become discouraged or dismayed.

Stay in the house!

If you want to be rescued . . . If you want God to move you into a future that will be marked by an abundance of life . . . If you want

God to create for you a place in His history . . . then don't move away from God. Stay in the house!

God's Word says, "He raises the poor out of the dust, and lifts the needy out of the ash heap" (Ps. 113:7–8). God expects you to stay raised out of the dust! Stay lifted up out of the ash heap. God did not bring you out of bondage to watch you go back into bondage. He is ordering your footsteps. He is working all things together for your good. Don't go back to the garbage pit out of which He raised you!

Wait Patiently for the Fullness of God's Timing. A day is as a thousand years with the Lord (see 2 Peter 3:8). God is not bound by man's concept of time. He is never early. He is never late. His timing is perfect. We may not understand His timing, but we must yield to it.

The promises of God come by faith *and* patience. Hebrews 6:12 says, "Do not become sluggish, but imitate those who through faith and patience inherit the promises."

There's no benefit to being impatient. There's no benefit in "making things happen." What you birth in the "flesh" you must maintain in the "flesh." However, what is born of God is managed and maintained by God.

It seems to us at times that God moves slowly. And oftentimes He does! He reveals His Word line upon line, precept upon precept. (see Isaiah 28:10 and 13). God moves deliberately, steadily, persistently, always moving in such a way that everything is in position for His purposes to be accomplished. God's Word says, "The Lord is not slack concerning His promise, as some count slackness, but is longsuffering toward us, not willing that any should perish but that all should come to repentance" (2 Peter 3:9). You may not see your deliverance on the horizon. You may not see the blessing that's on the way. But . . . your deliverance and your blessing are coming nonetheless. God is at work.

Stay in the house.

Stay in the house.

Stay in the house.

Because . . . once God brings you through your crisis, He will raise you to a new level of maturity and you will be *better* prepared and more fully equipped to enter into the fullness of His destiny for you. The pain of yesterday will pale in comparison to the pleasures God has for your tomorrow.

The day Rahab was delivered out of Jericho with all her family was the last day that Rahab was a harlot in a Canaanite fertility cult. God had a new life for her. She married Salmon, one of the spies, and they had a son named Boaz. Boaz became a wealthy, prominent man in the tribe of Judah. Boaz married Ruth, and their son was named Obed, who had a son named Jesse, whose son was King David. Rahab was the great-great-grandmother of King David. And in the centuries that followed, her descendant was Jesus Christ.

There's so much God has for you that you cannot begin to understand today. Stay in the house . . . and stay ready for the deliverance and the destiny God has for you.

When days of destruction come, it won't matter what the government does. It won't matter what happens in the economy or what happens to every other family in your neighborhood. It only matters whether you stay in the house!

Are you feeling confused today?

Are you feeling panic and fear?

Are you feeling that something is about to "change" but you don't know if it's a change for good or bad?

Deal with it!

Acknowledge that God is the Lord of the heavens and the earth. Receive Jesus as your Savior and put yourself under the covering of His shed blood. And then, stay faithful in your relationship with Jesus. Don't be moved from it. Begin to make the changes that Jesus instructs you to make. Get His vision for your life . . . and walk into that vision as He leads you!

ᕌ GOD'S WORD ON DORCAS

Dorcas lived in Joppa, a port city of the Mediterranean, east of Jerusalem. She was one of the first converts to Christ in the years following the resurrection of Jesus. She was a notable woman in the early church—not only did her life have a great impact on others, but there is also the fact that she was raised from the dead by Peter. The Scripture reference for Dorcas's story is Acts 9:36–42, and you will find it in the Appendix to this book.

4

DORCAS

"Everybody wants a bigger piece of me."

Dorcas is one of the most admirable women in the Bible. She is kind and giving. The Bible not only describes what she did, but the Bible gives us her *name*. Tabitha in the Hebrew language and Dorcas in the Greek language mean "doe" or "pleasant gazelle." Theologians believe she carried this name because of her inward and outward beauty—she was both physically and emotionally strong and graceful. She was a "got-it-together" woman.

She is called a disciple of the Lord Jesus. She was committed to the gospel of Jesus Christ. She was a deeply spiritual woman. She was full of good works, as a tree is full of fruit. Her good works gave her a reputation for being compassionate, resourceful, and generous.

Dorcas made coats and garments. Ministry is not just preaching and teaching. Ministry is also what you do in your daily routine to help others. God's Word says, "If a brother or sister is naked and destitute of daily food, and one of you says to them, 'Depart in peace, be warmed and filled,' but you do not give them the things which are needed for the body, what does it profit? Thus also faith by itself, if it does not have works, is dead" (James 2:15–17). Dorcas showed her faith by her works. Her faith was activated. She was taking care of the poor as her ministry.

Dorcas is the kind of woman we all seek out. She is the kind of woman who is especially sought out in times of crisis and great difficulty. The most trying times of life, of course, are the times of life that demand the most physical, emotional, and spiritual energy. The most trying times of life are the most draining times of life.

Dorcas was a giver. She was taking care of everybody else around her to the point of not taking care of herself.

Dorcas collapsed. She gave out. She died helping everybody but herself.

ARE YOU LIKE DORCAS?

Many women I know have done good to others to the detriment of their own selves. That's what we women do. We bring home the bacon and fry it up too. We make sure the kids get off to school, the bills are paid, the living room is dusted, the husband is happy, the boss is satisfied, and the church is clean.

Women today are under pressure as never before. They are expected to look like a million dollars, have their bodies in shape, have their minds perfected, be in tune with God . . . and still be a *Leave-It-to-Beaver* mother.

Today's women have more "conveniences" than ever before, but they also face more problems than their grandmothers and mothers faced. Unlike mothers fifty years ago, they aren't sending their children off to schools where the biggest problems are excessive talking and chewing gum in the classroom. Mothers today are sending their children to schools where drugs and guns are likely to be found. Wives today aren't dealing with husbands who are watching *Gunsmoke* on television, but with husbands who are bombarded by pornography on their computers at work.

Modern women also have more opportunities than women have ever had before. We have privileges and possessions in an abundance that's never been known up to now.

How does a woman face the pressures of a world filled with terrorism and uncertainty, and at the same time walk in perfect peace? How does a woman have the energy to get through a day that's packed with responsibility every minute of every hour, and at the same time, fast and pray? How does a woman take care of her man—looking good and smelling good—and at the same time, fry up the chicken for dinner? How does a woman take time to relax with her family, and at the same time get all the Christmas shopping done and make that homemade recipe to take to her mother-in-law's house? How can a woman have boundless energy and super strength and always be "up," while she's working eight hours a day and making sure the shopping cart isn't left in the parking lot?

The problem with Dorcas—and the problem with us—is that we help everybody and often hurt ourselves in the process.

What is it God would have us do? I believe God is calling us to audit our lives and then put our lives in balance. Our lives must be managed.

AUDIT YOUR LIFE

One of the questions I am asked most often is this: "How do you balance your life?" People look at my life and say, "You are a wife, a mother, a preacher, an administrator, a pastor, an evangelist, and a television personality. How do you do all you do?"

I have to audit my life.

In the financial world, an audit means balancing the deposits and withdrawals of money into your checking account. A "life audit" is very similar—it is taking a look at the deposits and withdrawals you have of your time, energy, creativity, commitment, and resources.

If there are more withdrawals than deposits, you are operating your life in the red, and sooner or later, something is going to break, fail, or fall apart. The damage may be to your health, to an endeavor you consider to be very important, or to relationships that you value highly. Making too many withdrawals and not enough deposits is going to leave you feeling "bankrupt"—empty, discouraged, and exhausted.

Know where you are physically, emotionally, mentally, and spiritually.

Know what God is calling you to do.

Know your limits.

How can you tell if you are weary and under pressure? One of the first signs is when you begin to overreact to things that you otherwise would have taken in stride. When things that used to roll off you suddenly become major issues, you are likely at the point of being weary and pressed. If you find yourself becoming overly critical of the least little mistake made by your child or spouse, if you find yourself reacting with rage at a driver who cuts you off on the freeway or a clerk who makes a mistake in ringing up your groceries, if little things begin to pluck your last nerve and you make mountains out of molehills, you are weary and pressed!

A woman who is weary and pressed feels she is just "existing" in a waste of days. When that happens, these are the sad results:

- She loses her joy. Life becomes totally bland. There's no zest or sparkle to a day. The result is there's less praise to the Lord. We must remember always that we are commanded by God to "rejoice in the Lord always! Again I will say, rejoice!" (Phil. 4:4).

- She loses her perspective. Things that aren't wrong may suddenly seem to be wrong, and vice versa—things that are wrong may suddenly seem to be all right.

- She loses her sense of doing any one thing well. She isn't the wife she'd like to be or that God has called her to be.

She isn't the mother she knows she should be or desires to be. She doesn't feel as if she's succeeding in any area of her life because she feels no joy, enthusiasm, or purpose for *anything* she is doing.

- She loses her gentleness. Life becomes one long series of frustrations and obstacles to be overcome. A hardness begins to develop in her heart and in her outward behavior. Her jaw becomes set.

- She becomes increasingly anxious and frustrated at every turn. She begins to have a furrowed brow, always worrying about what may strike her next. Yet Paul wrote to the Philippians, "Be anxious for nothing" (Phil. 4:6).

The woman who has no joy, no gentleness, and is anxious becomes her own worst enemy. Her biggest *enemy* is often her "innerme." She sabotages her own work and relationships. A bomb detonates because of what is on the inside. She is also more vulnerable to attacks from the enemy.

One of the strategies of the enemy is to wear us down. The enemy will battle you mentally, physically, and spiritually. His best chance of defeating you is when you are "weary." We must never allow ourselves to become ignorant of the enemy's strategies (see 2 Corinthians 2:11).

Most people can handle one battlefront with the enemy. Two battlefronts are more difficult. But three battlefronts are impossible. It's like a threefold cord binding your life, and the Word of God tells us a threefold cord is not quickly broken (Eccl. 4:12). The person who is hit with a boom-boom-boom attack of the enemy on all three fronts—mental, physical, and spiritual—is a person who is likely to become paralyzed. She is unable to function fully, to be effective, or to recover quickly.

AUDIT YOUR WEAKNESSES

You need to know your weaknesses. You can be assured that the enemy knows them, and that's where he will attack you first and most often! If you know your weaknesses, however, you can guard and protect those areas of your life even as you operate out of your strengths.

Mentally and spiritually, I am pretty tough. As a result, I can be like a spiritual locomotive heading down the track—focused, determined, and operating full-steam-ahead.

Physically, I am not as strong. The signals to me that I'm becoming weary or pressured tend to occur first in my physical body. My physical strength, therefore, is the area of my life that I must guard and protect.

In 1995, I traveled the world preaching the gospel. I went around the globe three times in just a few months and laid hands on more than a million people that year. The result? I found myself in an emergency room several times, so physically exhausted and dehydrated that I needed to be hooked up to intravenous fluids to restore my body. On one occasion, as he was hooking me up to an IV, an emergency-room physician said to me, "You'll feel better after you've had a bag or two of this." It took *seven* bags of fluid before my body said, "I've had enough." I was that dehydrated.

Why had this happened to me?

I thought God had called me to save the world. The Lord had shown me that I was to "shake nations"—but I was attempting to shake them all at once!

The Lord rebuked me and said, "Do you want to be preaching My gospel and praying for people twenty or thirty years from now?" My answer was, "Yes!" I truly want to be in ministry for the Lord, reaching more and more people ten, twenty, thirty years down the line if the Lord hasn't returned by then. I want to do as much as possible for the spreading of the gospel in my life. In saying "yes" to that question, I realized that God had not called me to shake all the nations in one day or one year. He had not called me to try to save the entire world in a day. I was to do what I could do to the best of my strength and ability . . . but I was not to go *beyond* the best of my strength and ability.

There is a huge difference between doing the work of the Lord to the best of your strength and ability and in striving to go *beyond* the strength and ability He imparts to you. Ephesians 4:7 states, "But to each one of us grace was given according to the measure of Christ's gift." God decides the degree or measure of gifting and allots grace to perform that calling accordingly. People ask, "How do you do it?" You "do it" because God gives you the grace for what He has called you to do. God works in you and through you, but you are always going to be a physical being—an earthen vessel—with limitations and frailties.

We must trust God to fill us, use us, and pour us out. But we err if we think we can go beyond the boundaries of our physical, human vessels to do things God never calls or requires us to do.

Something will signal you that you are going beyond the boundaries of what you should do, and are in need of restoration.

Be wise enough to heed the signals God gives you!

AUDIT YOUR STRENGTHS

It isn't enough to know your weaknesses; you must also know your strengths. As my husband, Randy, often says, "If the enemy can't get you in your weaknesses, he'll attack you in your strengths." For example, having determination and an inner drive to succeed is a good thing—it *can* be a strength. But at times, that determination/drive can be your undoing.

Know your strong abilities and gifts—those things that you

naturally do well. The ministry God has given you will draw on your God-given strengths. But, remember, your strengths are the areas in which you are likely to become exhausted. The enemy comes against us to wear us out when we are doing the right things!

As long as you are straddling the fence and have no purpose in your life, why would the enemy bother you? It's when you begin to work the Word into your life—sowing it into the fertile soil of your mind, accepting it in your heart, bearing fruit from it in your actions, and receiving a harvest from it thirtyfold, sixtyfold, and a hundred-fold—and to move in what God has promised you that the enemy will come against you to resist you (see Mark 4:2–20). When you begin to speak out the Word . . . that's when the enemy makes you a target to stop it from going forth. The enemy will make your life hard, and you will have to resist and press and fight against him to move forward. It's the resisting and pressing against the enemy that wears us out!

Yes, there will be trials, temptations, and tests that come your way. But God's Word says you must "count it all joy when you fall into various trials" (James 1:2). Why? Because those trials are a sign that you are doing good and the enemy is coming against you. And no weapon the enemy can throw at you will be effective in defeating you. Isaiah 54:17 says, "No weapon formed against you shall prosper." That's a promise of God! But—make no mistake—there *will* be weapons that are used against you.

Look at the example of Elijah. This great prophet of God took on 450 prophets of Baal in a spiritual showdown on Mount Carmel. The prophets of Baal prepared a bull for sacrifice and then cried from morning to noon, "O Baal, hear us!" all the while leaping about the altar and cutting themselves with knives and lances, but there was no voice and no response. They prophesied until the time of the evening sacrifice that Baal was going to answer their cries, but no answer came.

Finally, Elijah prepared an altar of stones with a trench around it and made ready a bull for sacrifice. He called upon the people nearby to drench the wood, the bull, and the altar with water until it filled the trench around the altar. Then he called upon the Lord and said, "Hear me, O LORD . . . that this people may know that You are the LORD God, and that You have turned their hearts back to You again" (1 Kings 18:37).

Immediately the fire of the Lord fell and consumed the burnt sacrifice, the wood, the stones, and the dust and licked up the water that was in the trench. The people fell on their faces, crying, "The LORD, He is God!" (v. 39).

Elijah called upon the people to seize the prophets of Baal, and he took them down to the Brook Kishon and executed them there—all 450 of them. Then he sent word to Ahab the king that rain was on the way to end the drought in the land. Elijah prayed from the top of Mount Carmel until his servant told him that he saw a cloud as small as a man's hand. Elijah then sent word to Ahab to prepare his chariot and make a dash for Jezreel before the rains came. Elijah "girded up his loins and ran ahead" of Ahab to the entrance of Jezreel (v. 46). He outran the king's chariot!

What a day of victory! What a day of doing well! Everything that Elijah had been doing was *good*. It was the Lord's work. It was done at God's command. It takes tremendous mental, physical, and spiritual energy to have a confrontation with evil in which the odds are 450 to 1. It takes tremendous energy to build an altar and prepare a sacrifice. It also takes tremendous energy to execute 450 prophets. It takes even more energy to intercede in prayer and still more to outrun a chariot to the entrance of a city. At the end of the day, Elijah was weary. He was physically, mentally, and spiritually exhausted . . . from doing good! He had exhausted himself so much that, as he sat under a juniper tree, he even asked the Lord to let him die (1 Kings 19:4). Exhaustion leads to confusion and carelessness.

Elijah was so drained from "doing good" that he put himself in a dangerous position.

Galatians 6:9 tells us, "Let us not grow weary while doing good, for in due season we shall reap if we do not lose heart." Most people I've met have never stopped to fully face the fact that they can grow very weary *doing good*. The more need they saw, the more need they tried to meet. The more need they tried to meet, the more exhausted they became trying to meet the need . . . and ultimately, the more weary they became.

Now that doesn't mean we should *stop* doing good. We just need to recognize that we are to keep ourselves from growing weary in the process. Otherwise, our tendency will be to give up. We need to pace ourselves daily as we do good, maintain "heart"—which means our joy, enthusiasm, and purpose—and keep our eyes on the truth of God that in His right season we will reap from what we are sowing.

Learn to focus on the seat of strength in your life. See what God has put into your life and what God requires of you. Focus on the vision God has called you to pursue.

Set your priorities accordingly.

AUDIT YOUR PRIORITIES

When I get to heaven, I will consider myself successful when these things happen:

- I know I will have been successful when the Lord says to me, "Paula, you did all I asked You to do. You fulfilled all the assignments I gave you."

My desire is to have the Lord say of me what was said of King David: "He raised up for them David as king, to whom also He gave testimony and said, 'I have found David the son of Jesse, a man after

My own heart, who will do all My will" (Acts 13:22). In David, the Lord found a person who did His utmost to complete all the assignments God gave him.

I want the Lord to say that same thing about me: "I have found Paula, a woman after My own heart, who did all My will."

- I know I will have been successful when my husband says, "Lord, You gave me the greatest wife ever." When Randy sings my praises that I have been a good wife to him, I will have accomplished that assignment of God in my life.

- I know I will have been successful when my children rise up and say, "I bless my mom." When my children call me blessed, I will know I have succeeded in that assignment of God. (See Proverbs 31:28.)

Fulfilling the call of God on my life, being the greatest wife I could ever be to Randy, and being the best mom I could possibly be will be the marks of greatest success to me.

Do I have friends? Some . . . and they are good friends.

Do I take time to nurture new friendships with the same time and energy I devote to my husband and children? No.

Do I spend a lot of time hanging out at the mall or going to lunch with casual girlfriends? No.

My foremost assignments from the Lord are my husband, my children, and my ministry.

I don't think it's going to matter if friends say, "Lord, Paula went to the mall with me," or "Paula and I had tea," or "Paula and I played tennis." Now, I'm not saying that going to mall, having tea with friends, or playing tennis are wrong. There are times when we need to relax with friends to balance out our lives—but when those things become confused with the greater priorities of our lives . . . when they detract from our greater purpose . . . when they water down or make less effective the efforts we put into our God-given vision . . . then we need to regain our focus on what truly matters for all eternity.

There are only so many pieces in a pie. There's only so much energy you can expend. There's only so much time you can allot. And there's only so much of yourself that you can give. And sooner or later, something or somebody is going to get the "crumbs" instead of a whole piece of pie. In nearly all cases, that "somebody" is the woman who is slicing up the pie and handing out the pieces!

Set realistic expectations for yourself. Know what you can do. Know *how much* you can do.

AUDIT YOUR MINISTRY TO YOURSELF

True ministry begins with ministry to the self.

Now, before you jump to a conclusion that I'm talking about a me-first attitude . . . I'm not.

The truth is, you can't lead a person to Christ unless you know Christ.

You can't preach the Word of God with power and effectiveness unless you have read and studied it.

You can't feed others if you don't have any food.

You can't give away what you don't have—and that includes time, energy, and creativity as well as money and material resources.

You can't minister "out" what hasn't been ministered "in." Jesus said, "If anyone thirsts, let him come to Me and drink. He who believes in Me, as the Scripture has said, out of his heart will flow rivers of living water" (John 7:37–38). Living water cannot flow out of your heart unless living water is present in your heart! If you aren't taking in all you can take in of Jesus, you can't overflow with Jesus to minister to others.

You can't love others unless you first love yourself. Jesus said, "You shall love your neighbor *as yourself*" (Matt. 22:39, emphasis mine; see also Leviticus 19:18). Jesus was saying we are to love people to the degree that we love ourselves. That means that you must love yourself as much as you love others.

Besides your relationship with Jesus, the most important relationship you can have is your relationship with yourself. What you believe about yourself and the way you treat yourself will determine what you believe about others and the way you treat them! Proverbs 5:15 tells you to "drink water from your own cistern, and running water from your own well." If you cannot drink from your own well of life, then you will never be able to help others. Ultimately we reach into our own wells to draw out what is in us in order to pour out to others.

You must begin to celebrate yourself. Only you know how far you have come to be the "you" that you are today! Recognize your own accomplishments. It is only then that you will truly be able to celebrate others, recognize how far they have come, and applaud their accomplishments.

AUDIT YOUR RELATIONSHIPS AND COMMITMENTS

Recognize that you can't be all things to all people. There are only so many people you can genuinely help at any given time in your life.

You cannot be "God" to another person. If there are people who always seem to be turning to you to solve their problems and meet their needs, be cautious. A person who is in perpetual need of *you* is a person who has more need of you than of God. You need to help that person begin to trust God to meet his or her needs, because only

God can be there all the time, for all eternity. There's a big difference between helping another person and "carrying" that person—trying to be that individual's all in all.

The Bible tells us about a lame man who was carried every day to the Beautiful Gate of the Temple (see Acts 3:2). Now, when a person is "carried" by others, that person yields all control to those carrying him. This man had turned over the responsibility of his life to other people. He had to go where they took him, do what they told him to do for as long as they told him to do it, and live according to their dictates. They carried him every day to the gate to beg. The men doing the carrying had the power to position him wherever they wanted him to be. From the lame man's perspective, he had allowed himself to become totally dependent on them.

The Bible never instructs us to turn all our problems over to another person. It instructs us to cast our cares upon the *Lord.*

The truth is, God wants each of us to trust *Him* as the source of our provision, direction, and healing. He doesn't want us to look to any person other than Him for our plan and purpose in life.

In like manner, God wants you to help others, but never take on the sole responsibility for their lives. God wants to have that position of responsibility so He can have that position of authority. He cannot be Lord if you are striving to be Lord.

God wants to work through you to help another person, but He never wants you to try to take on the role of the Holy Spirit or to be the end-all and be-all for another person.

Ask yourself, "Am I trying to fix another person?"

Ask yourself, "Do I need to be needed by that person? Is the need I'm trying to fill a need that the Lord desires to fill? Am I standing in the way of God doing His work in her?"

Sometimes you need to give your children over to the Lord . . . and let God be God in their lives.

You need to give your marriage over to the Lord . . . and let God be God in your spouse's life.

You need to give that situation at work over to the Lord . . . and let God be God in that situation.

Ultimately . . .

Only God is able to *always* be there for another person.

Only God is able to meet *all* needs.

Only God is able to heal, restore, deliver, and bring a person to wholeness.

AUDIT YOUR OWN MOTIVATIONS

Finally, it is important that you audit your own motivations for giving beyond normal human limitations. Why do you feel the need to drive yourself . . . to pursue perfection . . . to volunteer for the extra challenge? What are you trying to prove? To whom are you trying to prove it?

I meet so many people who don't believe God loves them, and they are striving to do things to win God's approval and love. They drive themselves beyond the line of "violation"—the line of warning that they are beginning to hurt themselves, harm their relationships, and destroy their peace.

The truth of God's Word is that He loves you unconditionally. He loves you regardless of what you do or don't do.

I know that if I never preach another sermon . . . never produce another television program . . . never participate in another conference . . . God will not love me any less. He loves me unconditionally as His daughter, not conditionally, based on anything I do or don't do.

Audit your own motivations and the reasons for your behavior. The greatest enemy may be the person looking back at you in your mirror.

Count the Total Cost. For a financial audit to be valid, all the costs need to be taken into consideration. That is true of a life audit as well.

I recently talked to a person who told me that for twenty-seven years, he drove two and a half hours *one way* to his workplace. That was five hours a day! I asked him, "Why did you do that?" He said, "The pay was better in one area; the living conditions were better in the other."

I thought to myself, *How much better? Was the pay 10 percent more? Twenty percent more? What was his time worth? What was it worth to himself, to his health, to his peace of mind? What was it worth to his family?*

The true cost of anything is not in dollars and cents. The true cost includes the amount of stress in your life, the impact on your health, the impact on the relationships you value, and above all, the impact on your spiritual life. When you take an audit of your life, consider *all* the costs.

Like an airplane, you can only carry so much weight. If you have too much baggage on board, you will be unable to soar.

TAKE RESPONSIBILITY FOR MANAGING YOUR OWN LIFE

It isn't enough simply to audit your life and to know your weaknesses, strengths, motivations, or to face up to your relationships, commitments, or habits that may be unhealthy. You must take responsibility for your own life and begin to *manage* your life according to God's principles.

What specifically are we called to manage?

We must manage our time, which means our schedules. We need to take a look at each day and say, "There are only so many hours. How can I use them best to pursue the priorities I have set?"

We must manage our energy. Some tasks and relationships take more energy—physical, emotional, and spiritual—than others.

We must manage our creativity. We must focus it for the greatest impact and effectiveness.

I've always had a pretty good sense of how to manage my life—my time, energy, and creativity. I know my limits. Life situations always teach us, however, more about balance.

Randy used to ask, "Who's the captain of your vessel?" Through the years he has reminded me often that I'm the captain of my own life. My decisions determine my destiny.

Jesus encountered a man lying by the Pool of Bethesda. The Bible says this man was "impotent" or "infirm"—the word means "ineffective." He was incapable of doing what life required. Jesus asked him, "Do you want to be made well?" The man gave an excuse for his impotency, blaming others for failing him. Jesus responded, "Rise, take up your bed and walk." He was saying to this man, "Master that which has mastered you. Don't blame others. Take responsibility for your own life and healing and effectiveness" (see John 5:1–9). Start mastering what is mastering you!

Have you ever been in a café and had a waitress pour you a cup of coffee as she said, "Tell me when"? If you don't tell her "when," she can pour until that cup overflows and coffee is all over the table. If you don't tell her "when," you can end up with a mess.

You have to learn how to say, "When."

People will keep dumping and dumping and dumping and dumping into your life unless you say, "No more!" Don't rely on others to notice when your cup is filled. *You* must be the monitor of your own needs and limitations.

Learn to Say, "No" and "Enough." You have a decision to make about every opportunity, challenge, or request that comes your way—say "yes" or say "no."

"No" is a complete sentence. If you want to be a little more polite in saying no, you might say, "No, thank you." But you must be firm in saying no when something that comes your way does not fall into your limited set of priorities and does not help you fulfill God's purpose for your life. You must be willing to say no regardless of who asks. You must say no when saying yes will cause a withdrawal of your time, energy, and commitment that cannot be balanced with an adequate deposit of time, energy, and commitment.

People tend to give added responsibilities and more work to people who are capable, who can do multiple tasks well, and who have a history of getting jobs done and done well. It's easy for women, especially, to be assigned more and more work for these very reasons. As an administrator, I am always looking for the most productive person to do a job.

There is a correct way to say, "Enough." There is a way to say, "I'm already committed and I cannot do the *best* job for you if I am stretched too far. Because I want to do the *best* job for you, let me take on only what I can do and do well." Point out the ways in which you are producing. Point out that you want to be a team player. But do not expect your boss at work, your spouse, or your children to recognize that you are taking on more than you can do. They won't see that you are overburdened! Only you can say, "Enough!"

Often the most difficult thing for a helper to say is, "I need help." That statement goes against human pride and against the thinking that *we* are indispensable to the success of any project we undertake.

As I said, Elijah felt that way. When Jezebel sent him a threatening message, Elijah ran more than a hundred miles to the south and then left his servant in Beersheba and walked a day's journey out in the wilderness desert and collapsed under a juniper tree and said, "It is enough! Now, LORD, take my life" (1 Kings 19:4).

When a person becomes weary, perspective becomes distorted. Elijah's did. He said to the Lord, "I alone am left" (v. 10). He thought he was the only righteous person left in the land and that he was all alone in having to do good. That's what weary people begin to believe. They believe, "I'm the only person capable. It all depends on me. And I just can't do it anymore."

"Nobody can do this but me" is a trap . . . but it's one many people routinely fall into! Women think that about their children, sometimes even when their children are forty years old! Women think that about their work. The truth is, if Dorcas had never made another garment after she was raised from the dead, *somebody* would have made garments!

Raise Up Helpers. Not only must you be willing to let others help you, but you must train up people who not only can *help* you, but who can one day *replace* you. That's the challenge of every mature parent . . . every mature leader . . . every mature Christian.

When Randy and I started our ministry, we each wore many different hats. Through the years as God enlarged our ministry and He led us to begin Paula White Ministries, I had to learn to release some of the responsibilities I once had at our church, Without Walls International. I had to release my responsibilities as the church administrator—there once was a time when there wasn't a check signed or a budget made that I didn't approve. I had to release my role in the children's church and the women's ministry. I had to release my participation in every Bible study the church conducted. The time came when I could no longer preach every Friday morning at the church and run every Bible study and supervise all administrative areas. I had to ask God who He had called and prepared to take on various positions, and then I had to train them and give them the authority to do the jobs that needed to be done.

Note that I asked God whom *He* was calling.

I poured good things into those people.

And I gave them the authority to do the job as God led *them* to do it.

Did each of these leaders do their jobs exactly as I had done them? No. But I had trained them well enough that I could trust them to move up to the next level of leadership God had for them, even as I was moving up to the next level of leadership God had for me.

Learn to Live a Balanced Life. Perhaps the greatest challenge we face in managing our lives is learning how to live a *balanced* life. Overloaded people fail. So do people who are out of balance in their lives.

Dorcas had a habit of making garments—it was a habit of doing good, but she was out of balance in doing good. She had a habit of doing good for others, but she did not have a *balanced* habit of doing good for herself.

Have you ever given so much encouragement to another person that you walked away from that conversation feeling drained and discouraged?

Have you ever helped somebody so much that you walked away feeling in need of help?

Have you ever given your best to a job or to a marriage and still walked away feeling battered and bruised and totally "spent" on the inside?

You can give so much life to others that you end up feeling dead inside.

The key to survival is a balanced life. So is the key to enjoying life to the fullest!

The enemy doesn't play fair. If you allow any area of your life to come out of balance, it's as if you are opening a door to the enemy. He moves into your life in the area that is out of alignment.

Balance Is a Learning Process. Experience is our greatest teacher when it comes to balance . . . *if* we will choose to learn from our experiences. We each have to *learn* to live in balance.

The beginning of that learning comes with a recognition that we are triune beings—spirit, soul, and body. The spirit has a need for both taking in nourishment and for giving out ministry. The mind has a need for both tranquillity and stimulation. The body has a need for both rest and exercise.

Part of finding balance is recognizing when a deposit or withdrawal is being made or needs to be made. People either make deposits into your life or withdrawals from your life. There's a season when God desires that we allow others to withdraw from us. But there's also a season when you need to connect with those who will make deposits into your life. In that season, you need to separate yourself from those who are drawing from you and draining you dry.

Every year I go to certain conferences or meetings where I do not preach. I don't even make an announcement, raise an offering, or say a prayer. I go to sit and soak up what God has for me. If I don't do that, I don't have enough "deposits" in my life. I get out of balance.

Years ago I decided that I did not have to have the perfect Hollywood body. But I did want to be healthy. The result is that I don't work out for hours every day; I work out three times a week. That's balance.

You need to find what works for you.

When you are in a situation that calls for you to be a pastor, be a pastor fully and effectively. When you are at home with your husband, be a wife fully and effectively. When you are alone with your children, be a mommy fully and effectively.

Don't try to be a pastor or a mommy when you are alone with your husband. Don't try to be a businesswoman when you are being a pastor. You have to know the role you are being asked to fill. And then rise up and fill it! God desires to give you the wisdom you need to restore balance if you have lost your balance. He also desires to give you the wisdom to maintain balance so you can be what you need to be *fully* and *effectively* in each situation in which He places you.

At times we face a need to rebalance our lives. We may need to readjust our priorities, change our habits, and find a new balance. Know what season of life you are in!

Give Yourself Opportunities to "Replenish" What Has Been Depleted. At times we need to rest. To rest physically means to sleep, to exert ourselves less, to attempt fewer physical chores. It might mean we need to go less and stay home more. To rest emotionally and mentally means to stop thinking about some things so much. It doesn't mean we stop caring, but it might mean we do stop caring *so much.* We turn our cares over to the Lord, asking the Lord to take care of the person in ways we cannot. To rest spiritually is to trust God to provide for us and others what we are wearing ourselves out trying to provide!

David said that the Lord was his Shepherd, who made him lie down in green pastures and led him beside still waters (see Psalm 23:1–2). God will sometimes make you lie down and be still. When He does that, He is trying to get you to the point where He can hook you up to His Holy Spirit in a way that will revive and rejuvenate your life!

After Dorcas died, her friends sent for the apostle Peter, who came immediately. The first thing Peter did was send everybody out of the room. There are times when you need to get away. There are times when you need to put everything and everybody aside for a little while in order to replenish and restore the areas that have been pulled apart or drained dry in your life.

I don't know the depleted area of your life. It isn't the same for everyone. If you are depleted spiritually, then you need to take time to replenish yourself spiritually. If you are depleted emotionally, you need to do those things that fill you up emotionally. If you are depleted physically, you need to do what's necessary to restore your body.

Allow Your Spirit to Be Restored. God not only replenishes us; He calls us to restoration. He wants us to be restored to full strength and effectiveness. Only God can restore our souls (see Psalm 23:3). We need to learn to come to Jesus and rest in Him.

In a parable, Jesus taught about a prodigal son who reached the point where he had "spent all." It was at that point that this son "came to himself" and said, "I will arise and go to my father" (see Luke 15:10–18). When you come to yourself and realize you have "spent all," the first thing you must do is go to the Father.

Jesus said, "Come to Me, all you who labor and are heavy laden, and I will give you rest. Take My yoke upon you and learn from Me, for I am gentle and lowly in heart, and you will find rest for your souls" (Matt. 11:28). Resting in your relationship with God heals a person of deep feelings of vulnerability, feelings of being overwhelmed, and feelings of exhaustion.

What does it mean to "rest" in the Lord? God "rested" on the seventh day of creation, not because He was tired but because He was setting into motion by example His desire that man experience restoration, replenishment, and refreshment. God designed us to work six days and rest one day. He designed us to have a rhythm in our lives in which we have a time totally devoted to restoring what has been given out, replenishing what has been used up, receiving back what has been spent, and refreshing what has grown stale. He designed us so that our deepest form of restoration, replenishment, and refreshment is to come in relationship to Him. We are to have a time for reexperiencing the fullness of the Lord's presence and power, renewing our fellowship with Him, restoring Him to the position of top priority in our lives. God designed us to have a day of praise and thanks and quiet meditation on His Word. He designed us to have a day in which we gather with others to praise and give thanks and to study His Word.

When we murmur and complain—which are signs of our unbelief—God must deal with our unbelief.

When we praise and give thanks—which are signs of our faith—God begins to deal with those areas of our lives that need His power, provision, and healing touch.

We have to walk in Him as our "Sabbath rest." As long as we are trying to run things our way, do things in our own strength, and accomplish our vision in our own ability, He cannot pour His strength and ability into us and through us. As long as we are striving to nourish ourselves, He cannot nourish us.

The psalmist cried out, "Restore to me the joy of Your salvation, and uphold me by Your generous Spirit" (Ps. 51:12). That's what happens when we go to God and say, "I have no strength, no joy, no gentleness, and too much anxiety." He will restore you.

At times, God's process of replenishment and restoration may seem slow. In those times, God's Word tells us we must "let patience have its perfect work, that you may be perfect and complete, lacking nothing" (James 1:4). We must continue to walk in our faith.

At times God's replenishment and restoration happen quickly. One of the amazing things about God is that He has a way of restoring to you in just a moment what may have taken a long time to erode or disintegrate. He is not bound by time.

We can know with great assurance that God desires to heal us and deliver us and preserve us and sustain us. The Bible says, "Blessed is he who considers the poor; the LORD will deliver him in time of trouble. The LORD will preserve him and keep him alive, and he will be blessed on the earth; You will not deliver him to the will of his enemies. The LORD will strengthen him on his bed of illness; You will sustain him on his sickbed" (Ps. 41:1–3).

God gives to the givers.

He takes care of the "carers."

He loves the lovers.

Hebrews 6:10 says, "God is not unjust to forget your work and labor of love which you have shown toward His name, in that you have ministered to the saints, and do minister."

But . . . God cannot give to you unless you put yourself into a position of receiving. You cannot receive restoration and minister to other people at the same time. There's a time for being ministered to and a time for giving out. The two cannot occur at the same time.

NAVIGATE YOUR COURSE

Why audit your life? Why manage your life? Why develop the right habits based on right priorities? Why seek to find the right balance in your life?

So you can navigate your life toward the destiny God has for you!

God doesn't desire that you merely exist; He wants you to live life to the fullest and to *go somewhere* in your life. You have a purpose. You have a destiny to fulfill. God desires for you to be effective in each situation in which He places you. You need to be replenished, restored, and strengthened to do what God still has ahead for you to do!

King Hezekiah once said, "This day is a day of trouble, and rebuke, and blasphemy; for the children have come to birth, but there is no strength to bring them forth" (2 Kings 19:3). A woman who is weary and paralyzed by the enemy's attacks is incapable of birthing the blessings God is sending her.

I believe strongly that God has a set, appointed time for your blessing, your breakthrough, your healing, your season. God finished you before He started you. Everything is marked on the calendar of God. But if you hit that set time that God has appointed for your blessing and you are too weary or too paralyzed to give birth, you can miss out on what God desires for you to have.

The promises of God are received in the spirit. It is in your spirit that you first receive God's vision for your life and gain an understanding of what God is calling you to be and to do. But it is in your flesh that those promises are "birthed" into the reality of this natural world. You have to have both the mental and the physical energy, strength, and ability to actually do what God calls you to do. You have to be able to do the work He sets before you to do.

When Peter spoke to Dorcas's body, he said one word: *"Arise!"*

God speaks that word to you today. To arise is to "stand up and bring forward." To arise is to "come into your being"—to become powerful, to come into the wholeness God has for you. Have you become a martyr to your marriage?

God's word to you today is "Arise!"

Have you poured yourself out for your children to the point of exhaustion?

God's word to you today is "Arise!"

Have you become stressed out by life?

God's word to you today is "Arise!"

Put death on hold. Turn to God and ask Him to restore your soul! Why audit your life? Why manage your life?

So you can move into your God-given destiny of ministry on this earth!

If you are feeling today that everybody is pulling at you, wanting a bigger and bigger piece of you . . . *deal with it* by allowing Jesus to show you how He wants you to adjust your priorities, your habits, and your relationships. Ask Jesus to give you the courage to say "No" and "Enough!" and to take on only those things that He asks you to do. Ask Jesus to replenish areas of your life that have become depleted and to restore your soul with His joy and His strength.

Now is the time to be strengthened and renewed so you can move forward into the fullness of what God still has for you to birth!

⌒ GOD'S WORD ON GOMER

Gomer was the wife of the prophet Hosea. God had com-
manded Hosea, "Go, take yourself a wife of harlotry." After
Gomer had given birth to two sons and a daughter, she
committed adultery and returned to a life of prostitution.
Again, Hosea bought her off the prostitute's slave market
and restored her to her role as a wife and mother. The
Scripture references for this chapter about Gomer are
Hosea 1:2–3; 2:4–5; and 3:1–3, and are found in the
Appendix to this book.

5

GOMER

"You just don't know how deeply I've been hurt."

Gomer was an exasperated, spent woman. She was dehydrated from life. She had been around . . . and around . . . and around . . . and around.

The Bible doesn't tell us what led Gomer to her life as a harlot. She was already in the sewers of sexual promiscuity when she stepped onto the pages of the Bible. We don't need to know the whys of her past. What we do know is that Gomer had been deeply hurt and traumatized. Something had happened to her that wasn't fair . . . wasn't right . . . wasn't good. But it had happened anyway.

What Gomer didn't know was that her circumstances were a setup by the enemy. The trauma that led her to a life of promiscuity was all a distraction to keep her from seeing her own awesome potential. Your circumstances also are hindrances to seeing God's abilities.

Gomer is like millions of women today who have been traumatized by something they didn't want to have happen to them . . . but it did. And now it is affecting every aspect of their lives.

Trauma refers to wounding. Just as the body can be traumatized or wounded, so can the psyche, the emotional and mental aspects of a person. The wounding of the psyche impacts a woman's feelings of security and well-being, her feelings of dignity, her beliefs about herself and her world, and even her will to live.

It would be a shame to die and never have lived. That type of existence is exactly what the enemy wants for you. He strives to penetrate the deepest facets of who you are (your heart, mind, spirit, and emotions) to throw you off your path to destiny.

TRAUMA HURTS THE HEART

A woman who has been traumatized can feel sorrow and a sense of loss.

Very often when distressed children are asked to draw a picture of the way they feel, they draw a heart that is wounded or broken in some way. Sometimes their drawings show a heart with tears or drops of blood flowing from it. Sometimes the heart has lines drawn through it or scribbled over it. Sometimes the heart is colored black. That's the way a woman can feel when she has experienced trauma.

God's Word tells us that Jesus feels our sorrows. The Bible declares that Jesus is our High Priest, who has a supernatural ability to "sympathize with our weaknesses" (see Hebrews 4:15).

Jesus feels what you feel.

Jesus knows how you hurt.

Jesus is capable of empathizing completely with your condition and your past wounding.

Jesus not only knows that you have been hurt, but He knows that you have *felt* hurt. He understands fully the wounding of your soul.

The prophet Isaiah described our Savior as "despised and rejected by men, a Man of sorrows and acquainted with grief." Isaiah said, "Surely He has borne our griefs and carried our sorrows" (see Isaiah 53:3–4). Because Jesus has felt what we feel, He is able to carry our sorrows for us. When we allow Jesus to carry our sorrows, it is then that we can be free of them!

The truth of God's Word to you is this: God wants to heal *your* hurting heart!

TRAUMA FRACTURES THE MIND

When you have been wounded, it affects your psyche in many different ways. Often, a woman who has been traumatized can't think clearly—she sometimes feels confused and scattered in her thinking to the point where she may feel as if she is going crazy. She sometimes can't remember things she once knew very well. She sometimes can't put two thoughts together in a logical or rational way.

Our lives move in the direction of our most dominant thoughts. The more you concentrate on the devastating experience, the more it will continue to eat away at your psyche and cloud your mind so that you cannot focus on anything else.

God cares a great deal about how we think! He wants us to be whole in our minds. God's Word tells us that we are to be "renewed in the spirit of [our] mind[s]" (Eph. 4:23). We are to think as Jesus thinks. The Bible tells us, "Let this mind be in you which was also in Christ Jesus" (Phil. 2:5).

His thoughts are to become our thoughts.

His creative ideas for our lives are to become our creative ideas.

His attitudes are to become our attitudes.

His opinions are to become our opinions.

The Bible calls us to "be transformed by the renewing of [our] mind[s]." With a renewed mind, we are to be able to "prove what is that good and acceptable and perfect will of God" (Rom. 12:2). In other words, we are able to know and understand God's plan for us. We are to be able to figure out what is good, versus what is evil. We are to be capable of perceiving and understanding what is acceptable behavior in God's eyes. We are to understand what God has called us to do and how He wants us to live.

The truth of God's Word is this: God wants to heal *your* fractured mind.

TRAUMA TAKES AWAY A SENSE
OF EMOTIONAL BALANCE

Most people know how to balance out the everyday stresses and strains of life. A person who has been wounded, however, often has a very hard time achieving emotional equilibrium. Balance can be very difficult to achieve and maintain. Simple things—such as everyday experiences, decisions, and problems that other people find routine— often become difficult to manage.

Something very small and insignificant to a person who has not been traumatized can send a traumatized person into a tailspin.

Something said in passing can be perceived as a tremendous arrow of injustice or rejection.

Something that may upset the average person for thirty seconds can ruin the entire day of a person who is emotionally wounded.

The truth of God's Word is this: God wants you to live a balanced life and to be whole spiritually, physically, and emotionally (see 3 John 2).

TRAUMA LOWERS SELF-ESTEEM

When you have been deeply hurt or emotionally bruised, your self-esteem always takes a hit. A woman who is traumatized feels "depersonalized"—less of a person. There's a stripping away of her self-identity and her self-worth. There's less of an understanding of her individuality, of what makes her unique. There's a feeling that her life has been irreversibly tarnished and diminished. She feels more vulnerable.

When we deal with others, we do so by reaching into our own well of self-esteem, and we treat them from that supply. When I first met my husband, I had very low self-esteem. I had a lot of issues to work through—things I had to "deal with." I said and did hurtful things to myself in those days, and in the process I hurt Randy. I never once intended to hurt him. My thinking was more, *I might hurt Randy, and rather than do that, I'm going to leave this relationship.* Leaving the relationship was a hurtful thing to me! I know this sounds absurd, but you create behavior that you fear the most. People who have been hurt tend to hurt others. While pulling Randy close to me, I was pushing him away out of fear that he would eventually leave me, which stemmed from my own insecurities. Because of those insecurities, my self-esteem was shattered. I believed that I actually deserved hurt and pain and brokenness. Out of that belief, behavior was created.

People with low self-esteem invariably hurt themselves. Sometimes they hurt themselves with substances that result in physical addictions, sometimes with emotional addictions, sometimes with eating disorders, sometimes with sexual sins.

A shattered person with low self-esteem feels helpless. It's very easy to develop a victim mentality—a mind-set that says, "I don't have any say in my life. I don't have any control over my choices."

Jesus came to *help* us. He came to give us an *identity.* He came to give us an opportunity to choose to live and be whole.

Trauma can lead a person to desperation . . . and desperate people do desperate things.

I don't know why Gomer made the bad choice she made to return to a life of prostitution. I don't know all the circumstances of her life that led her to become a prostitute in the first place.

I do know this . . .

No little girl grows up aspiring to become a prostitute. No little girl looks in the mirror and says, "I think I'll be a whore when I turn sixteen."

No little girl says to herself, *I'd like to be a woman who has deep emotional wounds. I'd like to become a woman who has deep anguish over old trauma.*

No little girl grows up thinking she's going to be divorced two or three times.

No little girl grows up thinking she's going to have to one day sell her body in order to put food on the table for her children.

No little girl dreams of growing up and becoming filled with despair. But desperate people do desperate things. And Gomer was a woman living in discouragement and depression and desperation.

BE CAREFUL WHAT YOU JUDGE

If I chose to live in judgment of all the people whom God has put in my life, I would have missed out on most of the blessings in my life, because most of the people God has sent my way have been like David's band of "misfits." They didn't "have it all together" in their lives. They didn't look or act right. But God said to me, "I will raise them up to be a mighty armor for you, to possess My promise to you. I have placed them in your path."

So many women in our world today face sickness . . . and someone comes to tell them, "There must be sin in your life."

So many women have hardships . . . and someone looks at them as if to say, "You must be reaping the consequences of your past behavior."

I refuse to make pronouncements like that over anyone's life!

I don't know what leads a woman to make the choices she makes. I don't know what led Gomer to do what she did. Only God knows how far Gomer had come. I do know, however, that we are not to play the part of God and be anyone's judge! Judgment belongs in the hands of God who is the only one who knows the heart of a person, "For the LORD does not see as man sees; for man looks at the outward appearance, but the LORD looks at the heart" (1 Sam. 16:7).

Don't Think Yourself Immune! Don't ever think you are immune from doing certain things. If you become desperate enough, you just may! You may find yourself with deep needs that go unattended . . . and at that point, you are likely to take desperate action. Don't ever think you would be above sleeping in a defiled bed if you were desperate to feed your starving children. Don't ever think you wouldn't enter a wrong relationship if you were desperate to feel love and to hear a kind word. Don't think you would be above doing some crazy thing if you were desperate to get attention or affection.

Even if you didn't do that desperate thing, you've possibly thought about doing it! Don't think you're exempt from anything! "The heart is deceitful above all things, and desperately wicked; who can know it?" (Jer. 17:9).

GOD CALLS US TO HEALING

God calls us to healing. And one of the mistakes we make about healing is that we think it is "forgetting." The truth is, we never fully forget what happened. Healing is not forgetting; healing is getting beyond the hurting. We know we are healed when we no longer live in the wounding of the past, when we are no longer trapped by the feelings associated with the wound. A wound is an event, but healing is a process. Don't bypass the process for the progress. The journey is important.

We are healed when we no longer keep changing the bandages or applying ointment or antiseptic to the wound. We are healed when God applies *His* balm of Gilead, the healing love and power of Jesus, over our wound and causes it to heal to the point that we have a scar that disassociates us from the pain we once felt.

I have a large scar on my right knee. That scar reminds me of an event in my life.

My brother is several years older, and throughout my childhood I craved his acceptance. I did lots of things to try to get his attention and win his love.

One day he and a friend were going fishing, and I decided that I wanted to go along. I grabbed a fishing rod and headed out after them, running through the woods to try to catch up. I was running hard and heavy, and I ran smack-dab into a boulder that got the best of me. My knee was split open—not just scraped or skinned. I had to be rushed to the hospital and have stitches. I lost a lot of blood, there was damage to the ligaments, and the pain was tremendous.

When I look down at that large scar on my right knee today I can remember that event in my life. I have a memory of it.

But . . . I feel no pain.

When God creates a scar over a traumatic event in your psyche, the same thing happens. You may have a memory of a terrible and painful event, but you are dissociated from that event by God's intervening love and healing power. You no longer feel any emotional pain associated with the tragedy. A scar reminds you that there was a wound, but it is now healed.

A person who has been healed of emotional trauma is able to say, "I recall going through that experience, and I know that it is a part of my past." However, the person is also able to say, "But I have no pain and I feel no emotional wrenching as I recall that tragedy."

A Scar Is Not a Mask. There's a huge difference between a scar and a mask. I encounter thousands of women every year who are "church women." They go to church regularly. Many have gone to church for years. But all those years, they have been wearing masks to hide the pain deep within their souls. They were wounded as children and as teenagers. Either through their own willful sins or, as in most cases, through the sins others have committed against them, they have been traumatized. And each has put on a mask to hide the pain.

That's hypocrisy. The word *hypocrisy* is a very old Greek word that related to the wearing of a mask during a theatrical performance. An actor would wear a happy face or a sad face—or sometimes a black mask or a white mask. The mask was used to convey to the audience what the actor wanted the audience to think.

That's exactly what we do when we put on a "happy face" and say that everything in our lives is just fine. We want people around us to think we are happy and whole. But inside . . . we are a mess. We are hurting and in raw pain. The wounds of the past have never been healed. They've been covered over not with a divine healing scar, but with a false mask.

We say to ourselves, *I don't want anybody to know that something bad happened to me when I was eight years old . . . I don't want anybody to know where I came from or what I did as a teenager . . . I don't want people to find out that I'm not really as good as I'd like for them to think I am.* We each put on a mask. We deal with other people in a superficial way. And all the while, we are hurting, hurting, hurting behind our masks. The wounds in our soul are open and gaping and infected.

We need to give ourselves and others around us permission to hurt and to express pain.

The expression of pain is part of the grieving process every person needs to go through after he or she has been hurt or suffered a loss. Grieving is vital to our coming to closure. Grieving is part of the healing process anytime we have lost something precious to us.

The loss may have been the loss of a loved one owing to rejection or death.

The loss may have been the loss of innocence.

The loss may have been the loss of virginity or the loss of a spouse.

The loss may have been a loss of self-worth, self-identity, or dignity.

A person who suffers any kind of loss needs to grieve.

Who can wipe a tear that will not fall?

The end of the book of Deuteronomy is all about grieving and closure. God knows that we need closure in our lives and He provides for it and allows it to happen.

The children of Israel had watched Moses go up the mountain to meet with God on numerous occasions. But one day when Moses was 120 years old, he went up the mountain and did not return. The Israelites had to come to the point where they accepted the fact that Moses had died on the mountain and would *never* return. God's Word says, "And the children of Israel wept for Moses in the plains of Moab thirty days" (Deut. 34:8). God knew the children of Israel needed to mourn the loss of their leader. He said, "It's OK for you to cry."

But . . . God also set limits on their mourning. He gave them thirty days, and then the verse concludes with, "So the days of weeping and mourning for Moses ended."

The next chapter in the Bible, the first chapter of Joshua, begins, "After the death of Moses . . ." God's plan called for the people to get up from their grief, draw to closure, and move forward!

There is a time for grieving . . . but then there is a time for the grieving to stop.

Move Through All *the Stages of Grief.* During the time the Israelites grieved, they no doubt experienced all the normal stages of grief:

- DENIAL. First, there's denial—"I can't believe this has happened." One form of denial is "escapism"—it's trying to escape so you don't have to deal with what has happened. The use of alcohol or drugs can be a form of escapism, an attempt to deny the pain of the past. You can't change what you don't acknowledge.

- ANGER. Second, there's anger that someone has hurt you or rejected you. "I'm angry that this happened to me. I didn't deserve it!"

- BARGAINING. Third, there's the bargaining stage—"If this happens . . . then . . . If God will . . . then I'll . . ." God doesn't bargain with us to allow us to stay in the past. He moves to heal us.

- DEPRESSION. Fourth, there's depression. There's a feeling that life will never be the same, and there's a longing for the former life.

- ACCEPTANCE. Fifth and finally, there's acceptance that what has happened, has happened.

After my father committed suicide, and my mother struggled to make ends meet, my life became a living hell. From the time I was six years old until I was thirteen years old, I was sexually and physically abused numerous times in horrific ways. Psychiatrists and psychologists have told me that, given what happened to me in those early years of my childhood, I should have been institutionalized for the rest of my life—I should never have been able to cope with what happened to me, much less be healed of it.

The truth is, I can't change what happened to me. There isn't anything I can do to take back the childhood I had. My father is dead. The abuse happened. That is the *past*. It's over. It's behind me.

I had to decide to move forward, and so do you. I had to come to the place where I said, "Paula, you can make that past a stumbling stone for the rest of your days or you can make it a stepping stone toward the future God has for you. You can live in a past that wasn't good or you can move toward a future that God says is good." I chose to move forward! And if I could make that choice, you can, too!

There are some things that may never be made "right" in your life. That broken marriage may never be restored. That lost relationship may never be found. Innocence and virginity cannot be recovered. Some things that are dead will not be returned to life.

Acceptance involves burying what is dead. It's leaving what is "over." It's not only accepting that the past was the past, but it's accepting that your future is still ahead of you. It's accepting the truth that God has a plan for your tomorrow. It's accepting the truth that God does not determine your future based upon your past.

That truth is so important for you to grasp—God never uses your past to determine your future. What was, was. What will be, lies ahead of you as a canvas with no paint on it. Let God design a masterpiece!

Don't Grieve Incompletely. It's important that you don't try to get to "acceptance" without going through the stages. It is only if you will go through all the stages that you are able to stand at the end of the process and say, "This happened. It hurt and I was angry about it. I no longer am trying to 'deal' with God about it. I've been depressed about it but I am no longer depressed. I accept this as a part of my history, but it is *not* a part of my future."

Acceptance allows a person to say, "I'm not a product of what has happened to me. I'm a product of what God says about me!"

Gomer hadn't drawn closure in her life. She had not fully grieved. She had not come fully to grips with her past so that she could move into her future. She *looked* as if she had drawn closure, but she hadn't.

The Illusion of Having "Arrived." By the time we are introduced to Gomer, she's a cleaned-up, respectable wife and mother. Gomer had finally arrived. She was the wife of a prophet, a mother of children.

Nobody who had known her fifteen years ago was likely even to recognize her now. Nobody in polite society would ever have believed how far she had come to be a respectable woman. Nobody who saw her in her life as a wife and mother would have ever guessed she was once a woman of the night—a whore.

Gomer was caught between who God had called her to be and who she used to be. She had one foot in her past and one foot in her present. She had changed her social status on the outside, but she hadn't changed the way she perceived herself on the inside.

How do we know this? Because when a crisis hit Gomer's life, she went back to her old patterns. Something triggered a response in her, and she ran to her past. A woman who has been traumatized and hasn't fully grieved over that past and drawn closure on it does just that. She runs to the familiar. She reacts in the old way. She follows the old pattern. She resorts to the old self-sabotaging, self-destructive behaviors. She continues to hurt herself.

HEALING IS A PROCESS OF CHANGING

Trauma changes you. Healing also changes you. In fact, the Bible tells us that God turns around trauma for our good. What once was so exceedingly painful and horrible can become by God's power a driving force that produces very positive results! The Bible tells us, "All things work together for good to those who love God" (Rom. 8:28). The Bible also tells us that we can say to the memory of any person who caused us trauma, "You meant evil against me; but God meant it for good" (Gen. 50:20).

God's ultimate plan for you is *always* good.

NOW Is the Appointed Time. God has an appointed time for healing everything negative that you have been through in your past. It doesn't matter what happened, when it happened, or where it happened. God has a *now* word to heal a past wound.

He has a *now* word to touch a past event—to bring it into today and heal you right where you are.

God wants to create a scar over any wound in your life—to heal that wound so that it is "covered over." He wants the bleeding, the infection, the pain, the oozing, the wounding to stop!

Wounding was an *event*.

Healing is a *process*. It is much like "baking." It involves a lot of steps and ingredients. But if you put all the ingredients together in the correct order, you get the right result!

Forgiveness is the first step in your healing process—but we must make certain that we aren't taking on "sins" that aren't ours.

Our Sins Versus the Sins of Others. Emotional trauma comes to us from two sources:

One, our own sins traumatize us.

Two, the sins of others traumatize us.

We must ask God to forgive us for those things that we have done to ourselves. We need to ask God to forgive us our sins.

We must ask God to heal us of those things that we could not prevent and never deserved. We must also ask God to give us the grace to forgive those who have sinned against us and let go of the bitterness and pain they caused us. We must allow the love and acceptance of Jesus to fill our broken, damaged, fragmented hearts and make us whole.

One of the issues involved here is an issue of personal responsibility. We *must* take personal responsibility for our own behavior. Some actions on our part can lead to very bad consequences. We can't lay everything at the feet of another person . . . or an institution . . . or even the devil . . . and say, "He made me this way." "They caused me to end up here." "The devil made me do it." In many cases, *we* are the ones who made our own bad choices. *We* are the ones who charted a very negative course for our lives. *We* are the ones who listened to the devil's voice and acted out his temptations to us.

Get honest with yourself and take responsibility for your life: "I did it. I was wrong. I messed up. I rebelled against You, God. I was in disobedience to You. Please forgive me."

God's Word says that God's grace is "sufficient" (see 2 Corinthians 12:9). There isn't any sin you've committed, mistake you have made, or weakness you have manifested that can't be forgiven. First John 1:9 tells us, "If we confess our sins, He is faithful and just to forgive us our sins and to cleanse us from all unrighteousness." There's no sin beyond the boundaries of His faithfulness to forgive.

Walk Away from Those Things That Aren't Your Responsibility! We are *never* to take on the responsibility for another person's failures or sins against us.

If another person has been cruel to us . . . we must stand up on the inside and say, "That person was cruel. It had absolutely nothing to do with me or anything I did. What that person did came out of his [or her] own dark heart. I did nothing to deserve or warrant their cruelty."

If another person rejects us, we must come to the place in our own hearts and minds that we say, "That person obviously could not discern my true value and worth. Her actions had nothing to do with who I really am. She was the one with the problem!" Recognize that those who reject you have no ability to see inside you.

If another person abuses us, we must come to the place where we know with certainty, "That person was wrong in what he did. I did absolutely nothing to deserve such horrible abuse. The abuse came from his own sinful heart."

Guilty over what we truly do in open rebellion against God . . . yes.

Guilty over what someone else does to us in his or her rebellion against God . . . never!

Guilt Can Hold You Back. Guilt is one of the foremost things that can cause a woman to believe God can't or won't use her.

Our feelings of guilt, in turn, cause us to say to ourselves, "God couldn't possibly love me because He allowed a bad thing to happen to me." And because a bad thing happened *to* us, we then conclude, "God can't possibly use me because I've been a participant in bad things!" A very negative cycle of erroneous thinking can begin to churn in our spirits. We believe more and more that we are unworthy of God's love and His "use" for us as Christians.

Nothing could be farther from the truth of God's Word!

You must choose to receive God's forgiveness in your life and choose to move forward.

Bury what is dead. Leave what is "over." Get on with what God has for you! The Bible gives us a tremendous example of this in 2 Samuel 12:16–23: King David pleaded with God for the life of the baby that had been born to Bathsheba. God's Word tells us that David "fasted and went in and lay all night on the ground." David was in deep anguish—his heart was broken.

But when his servants came to him and told him that the child was dead, David "arose from the ground, washed and anointed himself, and changed his clothes; and he went into the house of the LORD and worshiped. Then he went to his own house; and when he requested, they set food before him, and he ate."

David's servants were puzzled at his behavior. They said, "You fasted and wept for the child while he was alive, but when the child died, you arose and ate food."

David said, "While the child was alive, I fasted and wept; for I said, 'Who can tell whether the LORD will be gracious to me, that the child may live?' But now he is dead; why should I fast? Can I bring him back again? I shall go to him, but he shall not return to me."

You may have wept in anguish before God. Your heart may have been broken. You may have fasted and prayed. And in spite of anything you did or didn't do . . . God said no to that relationship, no to that miracle you wanted, no to that outcome you desired.

When God's answer is "no," you must decide to say "yes" to the future He holds out to you. You must *get up*. David arose!

Who knows what good things God has for you in your future? Who knows the abundance of life He has for you? You *won't* know unless you rise up and walk toward your future!

Get up and pray.

Get up and read the Word.

Get up and take action!

TO OVERCOME YOUR CONDITION, KNOW YOUR POSITION!

Gomer never fully accepted the truth that she was forgiven. She never accepted her new position in life. Gomer continued to live in shame.

"Shame" is what other people put on you. People called Gomer "harlot." They labeled her life by what she did as her profession. And because they saw her profession as being shameful, they saw Gomer as being shameful.

But how did *God* see Gomer?

What name did *God* have for her?

Names in the Bible have great significance and Gomer's name means "beloved."

God saw Gomer as His "beloved!" That was her position in His eyes. God did not call Gomer by her shame. He called her according to whom she belonged, not what she did or had done.

God calls you by your position in Him . . . not your condition of shame.

God calls you by your *name* . . . not by your pain.

He says to you, "You are mine! You belong to me." And all that matters is Who you belong to . . . not what you've been through.

Don't Let Others Define You. You cannot stop other people from trying to put labels on your life. But you can keep those labels from sticking to you!

People will always try to define "who" you are by what you do—including how you dress, how you talk, and how you act. I get a letter almost every week from somebody who sees me on television and writes to say, "Why do you preach the way you preach? Why do you talk the way you talk? Why do you dress the way you dress?" They want to refine me in some way to meet their standards. Some people seem to think I've just recently started preaching, talking, and dressing the way I preach, talk, and dress. The truth is, I'm a girl from Mississippi and I've been talking like a Southerner all my life. I've been dressing and preaching the way I dress and preach for a very long time! That's who I am, and I'm not interested in living up to other people's expectations of me. I'm interested only in living up to what God calls me to be! If I had accepted the labels life had put on me, I'd never be who I am today. If I had allowed what had happened to me to define who I was, I'd never be what I am and where I am today!

If you allow other people to define you, they'll limit you—they'll define you in a way that is less than what God has for you. They'll define you as less successful than God wants you to be. They'll define you as less blessed, less intelligent, less effective, and less spiritual than God wants you to be. If you allow them to define you and limit you, you truly *will* be limited! You won't press forward into the fullness of what God says you can be.

Don't ever accept any nonsense that others speak over you.

Accept only what God says about you, and the words of those who align themselves with His proclamations over your life!

God defines who you are by Whose you are.

I have two words for you to use when the enemy brings your past to your remembrance: *So what?*

The next time the enemy says, "You can't be the head; you'll always be the tail" and others accuse you by saying, "Look at the life you led," respond, "So what?"

The next time the enemy says, "You can't get that loan or buy that house or start that business or have that job or go to that university—you have a past," respond, "So what?"

The next time the enemy says, "You can't have a good marriage; just think how you lived in the past," respond, "So what?"

So what does your past have to do with your future? In God's eyes . . . your past has *nothing* to do with your future!

God Calls You "Beloved." When Gomer returned to harlotry, Hosea could have said, "This woman hurt me . . . humiliated me . . . failed me . . . even backslid against God." He could have left her on the auction block. But he didn't. You see, Hosea's name means "salvation." And in the fullness of his identity, Hosea emptied his pockets and bought Gomer, the beloved, back to be his own.

Jesus didn't leave you in your condition either. He emptied His life on the cross and bought you back. He is your Savior. He calls you "beloved."

Unconditional love chases a person down. It seeks out the person who is bent over and can't stand up. Jesus saw a woman in the synagogue one day. God's Word tells us, "There was a woman who had a spirit of infirmity eighteen years, and was bent over and could in no way raise herself up" (Luke 13:11). So many women are in that position. They are bent over, unable to raise themselves up. Life has overwhelmed them and "bent" them. This woman didn't go to Jesus or call out to Him. She may have been bent over to the degree that she couldn't raise herself up enough even to see Him. Jesus called out to her! The Bible says, "When Jesus saw her, He called her to Him and said to her, 'Woman, you are loosed from your infirmity.' And He laid His hands on her, and immediately she was made straight, and glorified God" (Luke 13:12–13).

The same love that God showed the "bent" woman suffering an infirmity, is what He so desperately wants to share with you today. The question is whether or not you can accept it.

God loves you.

He is pursuing you.

He is chasing after you with His love.

How difficult it must have been for Gomer, who had been passed around as an object of little worth, to believe that someone could find her valuable.

One of the greatest challenges in life is to accept the unconditional love of God. How can we receive unconditional love after we have been wounded by trauma?

The first step in receiving is to say to yourself, "I will not base my actions on *feelings*. I will base my actions on what God's Word says." In my own life, it didn't matter whether I "felt" God loved me. God's Word said He loved me and loves me and will love me! I had to choose to believe what God's Word said and put more of my trust in that, than in my own feelings.

You must also face your fears, including your fear of love. You would think that a person who deeply wanted love would not be afraid of love, but the exact opposite is often true. Many times, a person who has been deeply hurt builds high walls, and there's a fear of anything that comes "too close." Receiving love requires a degree of vulnerability, and vulnerability is very difficult for a wounded person. I had to say to myself, "I will not fear love." It's hard to face a fear, but we *must* face our fears if we are to overcome them. I had to say,

"So what if I feel a little vulnerable? I will take the risk. I will not give in to the fear that might keep me from the love I long to experience."

You must take a risk in reaching out. You must come to the place where you say, "Just because one man hurt me doesn't mean all men are going to hurt me. Just because one man left me doesn't mean all men are going to leave me. Just because one man abused me doesn't mean all men are going to abuse me."

You must begin to praise God for the truth that He has already accepted you. It's done! You don't have to do anything, act a certain way, dress a certain way, or speak a certain way. You are *in* the Beloved even if nobody else on this earth accepts you or loves you.

Your position in Christ is not only that of "beloved," but "redeemed."

God Calls You "Redeemed." Gomer didn't go in search of Hosea after she had gone back to harlotry. Hosea went in search of her! Can't you just see this dignified prophet of God saying to himself, "She must be out to lunch with the maid" . . . "she must have gone to have her nails done" . . . . "she must have gone to the market" . . . "surely she couldn't have gone *there.*" But he went to find her, and when he found her, she was on the block as a prostitute. She once again made herself available for sale as a whore. And Hosea bought her. He redeemed her.

Jesus has redeemed you. It's already an accomplished fact. We *have* redemption through His blood and forgiveness of our sins according to the riches of His grace. Not *shall* have, but *have* (Eph. 1:7). *Have* is a possessive term that means, "It's mine. I possess it . . . right *now.*" To redeem is to regain possession by repurchase. It means to rescue or deliver. It means to pay a ransom to free a person from bondage. That's what Jesus did for you on the cross. Jesus redeemed you and you *are* delivered. You *are* free. You *are* rescued from your sin. The past is the past. It's over.

God has no desire to keep from you His plan and purpose for you. The very opposite is true. He wants to reveal and make known to you all that He has done for you and all that He has destined you to be. Ephesians 1:7–9 says, "In Him we have redemption through His blood, the forgiveness of sins, according to the riches of His grace which He made to abound toward us in all wisdom and prudence, having made known to us the mystery of His will, according to His good pleasure which He purposed in Himself." What God has predestined for us, He desires to make known to us.

The quality of your life depends on your knowing what God has done for you!

It is knowing your position in Christ Jesus that gives you the power to overcome any condition related to your past. When you know your position, your old "condition" has no power over you.

The moment you begin to understand the mystery of God, and when His plan for your life begins to be unveiled before you, you will have a new energy flowing through you. You will have the power to straighten up on the inside and on the outside. You will have a new posture, a new bearing, a new dignity. When you begin to understand who loves you and who has adopted you into His family, you'll have a new identity, a new strength.

Are you aware that the Lord has a position for you? Are you living in that position?

God Calls You "Useful"—He Has Something for You to Birth! God redeemed you for a reason. He redeemed you for a purpose. He redeemed you so you can fulfill His assignment for your life. God sees you as useful. He has a mission for you to accomplish!

God's Word says that we were "predestined" to adoption by Jesus Christ to Himself (see Ephesians 1:5). *Pre* means "before." The word *destined* means "end." That means that before you began—even before you were born—God had designed your "end." He finished you before He placed you on this earth. He designed you from start to finish.

Even before anybody else accepted you, He accepted you.

Even before anybody else loved you, He loved you.

God's Word says, "Before I formed you in the womb I knew you; before you were born I sanctified you" (Jer. 1:5). God gave you the color of eyes you have. He gave you the color of skin you have. He gave you the DNA that you have—your genetic makeup. He gave you the intelligence that you have, the ability to commune that you have, the personality you have. God designed you *perfectly* for the assignment on your life.

You must *believe* that to be true!

Many women have a dream. But they don't have the strength to "deliver" that dream, to birth it into reality. Where do we get that strength?

The strength for what we *do* flows out of what we think or believe we are capable of doing. We simply don't attempt things that we don't think we can do. That's why the apostle Paul's statement to the Philippians is so powerful—"I can do all things through Christ who strengthens me" (Phil. 4:13). Here was a man who was in prison, for much of the time chained between Roman guards. Yet he proclaimed, "I can do all things!" His self-esteem was rooted in Jesus Christ. He saw Christ as enabling him completely to do everything in his life that really mattered. He saw his life as being one of strength and ability and of continually renewed opportunity!

Paul didn't look around and say, "Oh, I can't do that. I won't even believe for it." No! He said, "I *can* do *all* things through Christ."

I know many people who are quick to proclaim, "God can do all things." They believe that God has unlimited power and ability and wisdom.

What they do *not* proclaim is, "God can do all things *through me."* They don't believe God can use them, or that He *will* use them. They do not see themselves as being people whom God can use for His glory.

Are you saying "I can!" today?

Do you truly believe that God wants to use you? Your believing will give you the strength to give birth to God's promise!

The Doors Set Before You. God is setting some doors in front of you. The sign on door number one says LIFE and GOOD and BLESSING. The sign on door number two says DEATH and EVIL and CURSING (see Deuteronomy 30:15).

God's Word challenges us, "I call heaven and earth as witnesses today against you, that I have set before you life and death, blessing and cursing; therefore choose life, that both you and your descendants may live; that you may love the LORD your God, that you may obey His voice, and that you may cling to Him, for He is your life and the length of your days" (Deut. 30:19–20).

God gives you a chance to make a choice. But He tells you which choice to make!

It's up to you to choose His choice!

You have to shut the door to disobedience.

You have to open the door to obedience.

The consequences of your choice are not limited to your life—they impact the lives of your children as well. The truth of God for you and your family today is this:

No matter what you went through . . .

No matter what you *didn't* go through . . .

God calls you to leave the past and press toward the future He has designed for you. He says to you, "Today is a new day!"

Choose what gives life.

Choose what is good.

Choose what produces blessing.

Every time you see the sunrise of a new day, praise God! He's given you another chance! He's given you another chance to fight forward . . . to proclaim every promise He has . . . to grab hold of your destiny . . . and to live life to its fullest!

It's OK to hurt. But you must heal and move forward. If your past pain is hindering you in any way . . . *deal with it* by allowing Jesus to heal you in every place you hurt! Allow God's love to pierce through your pain! Don't let your history hinder you from your destiny! Hear the sweet voice of a loving gentle Savior calling you today! He is calling you by your name, and not by your shame! It is His love that draws you and pours a "balm of Gilead" on every open wound to restore you, mend you, heal you, and hold you! Yes, you have been hurt. But now is your time to *heal!*

⌒ GOD'S WORD ON HANNAH

Hannah lived in the hills north of Jerusalem, where she was one of the two wives of Elkanah, a devout man who regularly worshipped at the tabernacle in Shiloh. Hannah pleaded with God to give her a son, and she gave birth to Samuel, who became the high priest and judge of Israel. The Scripture reference for Hannah's story is 1 Samuel 1:1–20, and you will find it in the Appendix to this book.

6

HANNAH

"I can't stand that woman!"

Hannah was a blessed woman. In fact, her very name means "favored" or a woman with special advantages. She was a woman who was endowed with special gifts. She was provided preferential treatment. She had a man who loved her and she was financially secure. She "had it going on!" But, she also had an adversary by the name of Peninnah who "provoked her daily" with the fact that she was barren. Have you ever wondered why women fight women? Why, no matter where we are in life, there always seems to be an adversary to battle?

As Charles Dickens wrote in *A Tale of Two Cities,* "It was the best of times, it was the worst of times." Although Hannah was very blessed, the Bible says she desired a child and her womb was "shut"— she was barren. Hannah had it together in so many areas of her life, yet in other areas of her life, she was hurting.

Have you ever been there? Have you ever known what it means to have things going right in many areas of your life, yet in one or more areas, things couldn't be going more wrong? Have you ever known what it means to live in the best of times and the worst of times . . . at the *same* time? Have you ever been on the mountain and in the valley at the same time—perhaps to have your career soaring even as your marriage is falling apart, or to have your ministry going great just as your husband is laid off at work, or to have your family life strong but not have enough money to feed your children, or to have your husband loving you and sending you roses even as your body is diagnosed with a terrible disease? Have you ever been in that place where you appear on the outside that you are succeeding, and yet on the inside, you are fighting a horrific battle? That's what was happening in Hannah's life.

DIVISION IS A DEVICE OF THE ENEMY

The conflict between Hannah and Peninnah is very telling because it represents any area of division in your life that may be distracting you from your walk with God. We'll get to the fact that this is a classic case of female rivalry, but first, let's examine the fact that there was division at all in the home of a devout man of God. Does that surprise you? It shouldn't. Take it from me; people who love God and lead blessed lives can still have problems. People can praise the Lord in church . . . and go home to a spouse who acts like the devil. People can be part of a "team" . . . and still feel left out. People can be part of something . . . and not have it be part of them. People can be devout . . . and still be divided.

God's Word asks, "Can two walk together, unless they are agreed?" (Amos 3:3).

Division is one of the devices of the devil. Paul said to the Corinthians, "We are not ignorant of his devices" (2 Cor. 2:11). The Bible tells us the devil's tactics are intended to steal, kill, and destroy (John 10:10). Divide-and-conquer is a preferred strategy of the devil. The devil doesn't just want to give you a flat tire or a bad hair day. He wants to cause you to have a divided mind. He wants to see your heart shattered into a million pieces so that you will never get your life together again. The enemy knows that with a divided mind and broken heart, you will question the fundamentals and foundations of your faith and keep asking, "Where is God?" and fail to reach your destiny. The devil wants you to be so broken and busted and bankrupt in your life that you are totally empty physically, mentally, emotionally, and spiritually.

The devil comes to divide you and break you personally. He also comes to divide and break your family. He comes to divide and break your church. He comes to divide and break all your relationships. We know we are broken and divided when . . .

we can't get along with our husbands,

we can't get along with our children,

we can't get along with our mamas,

we can't get along with our fathers,

we can't get along with our employers or coworkers,

we can't get along with our pastor or that brother or sister who sits on the other side of the church.

We may be devout . . . but we are divided.

And where there is no unity, there is strife.

That's why Jesus prayed earnestly for His disciples, "Now I am no longer in the world, but these are in the world, and I come to You. Holy Father, keep through Your name those whom You have given Me, that they may be one as We are" (John 17:11).

Walking in Unity Isn't Easy. It takes effort, diligence, and labor. That's what the word *endeavoring* means in Ephesians 4:3. What is the work we are to do? It's the work of staying in the Word, meditating on it day and night. It's the work of staying in Christ, trusting Him, and looking to Him daily to do His work in you. It's the work of walking daily in the Spirit.

God is love, and if we are filled with God's Spirit, then we can't help but love. Love will be our automatic response (see 1 John 4:15). God's Word says, "If someone says, 'I love God,' and hates his brother, he is a liar; for he who does not love his brother whom he has seen, how can he love God whom he has not seen?" (1 John

4:20). Bitter waters and sweet waters cannot flow out of the same fountain (see James 3:11). If we are walking in the Spirit on a daily basis, love will flow from us.

We are to endure, stand firm, and *love!*

Love Covers a Multitude of Sin. Love will allow you to live in a way that looks beyond sin and sees grace (see 1 Peter 4:8). Love motivates you to stop talking about people and start praying for people. When you get connected to another person in prayer, you can't help but develop compassion for that person. And what is compassion? Compassion means loving another person with the foreknowledge that he or she will hurt and disappoint you. Compassion is loving another person *in spite of* his weaknesses in the flesh, knowing that you also have weaknesses in the flesh. You never know what weakness in him might appear on Monday . . . or what weakness in you might show up on Tuesday . . . just pray that your weakness and his weakness don't show up at the same time on Wednesday!

Love doesn't dismiss sin as sin—no, it "covers" sin with understanding, with compassion, with a humble admission that "there, but for the grace of God, go I." Love covers sin with a willingness to say, "I'm sorry."

Why is it so hard for a person to say, "I'm sorry"?

Pride.

We make all sorts of excuses: "He never says he's sorry, so why should I say I'm sorry?" "I was right, so why should I say I'm sorry?" "Sorry doesn't mean anything, so why say it?" That's wrong thinking. It doesn't matter what the other person says or doesn't say. If you are going to be loving as Christ loves you, you will say, "I'm sorry" a thousand times if you need to. If you can't say you're sorry, you'll only *add* to the strife and confusion.

God's Word says, "For where envy and self-seeking exist, confusion and every evil thing are there" (James 3:16). Pride is at the root of envy. Pride is a total self-seeking attitude. Where pride exists, confusion and evil erupt.

Confusion is instability, a state of disorder. Disunity means to move away from oneness. If you want to know why your household is in a mess, it's because there's confusion and instability there. Why? Because there's pride instead of love.

Strife produces contention, anger, pain, hate, bitterness, resentment, and a total lack of peace.

When you decide to walk in pride, confusion, and strife, you are opening the door to the devil. And when you open the door to the devil, you don't get to pick and choose which form of evil comes your way. You can't say, "I'll take lust, but not murder" or "I'll take greed, but not hate." The devil is given legal authority to do what *he* chooses when you make the choice to not to walk in unity. When you don't walk in love, you open the door to *every* demonic spirit and influence.

Division Is Often a Man-Made Problem. The problem in Elkanah's home was not a devil-made problem. The devil *used* the problem . . . but the problem was mostly man-made.

I don't think it takes a brilliant mind to conclude that the main reason for Elkanah's family to be divided was this: there was one man and two women in this house. Any time you have one man and two women, you'll have problems.

Most theologians believe Elkanah most likely married Hannah first, but when she didn't have children right away, he married Peninnah, who gave him children. Men are often beaten with the rods of their own making. In many ways, Elkanah brought this problem of a divided family on himself. Our decisions determine our destiny.

Why do we make bad decisions? Because we don't seek God's wisdom before we make major decisions and choices. We don't go to

God and ask for His opinion and His direction. We don't go to other godly mentors and counselors for advice. God's Word says, "In the multitude of counselors there is safety" (Prov. 11:14). We are wise to seek godly counsel before we make *any* major decision in our lives. We are to pray and wait and watch until we have God's wisdom.

Every action has a reaction, and if we don't get God's wisdom, we are very likely in our own flesh to take actions that bring about a negative reaction.

God's Word tells us that Hannah and Peninnah were in contention. They were in strife. There was no unity and no love flowing between these two women. The Bible says that Peninnah "provoked her [Hannah] severely, to make her miserable" (1 Sam. 1:6). To *provoke* is to violently agitate. Peninnah kept Hannah shaken on the inside. To be provoked means to have an inner rage that threatens to erupt at any point—Hannah lived at the point of "losing it."

JEALOUSY IS ROOTED IN FEAR

What was the real situation here? Hannah had a man in her life who loved her dearly but didn't understand her. She had a woman in her life who understood her completely but didn't love her.

We women need to be both loved *and* understood.

This brings us back to the question of why women fight women. A female rivalry is nearly always rooted in jealousy. And virtually every woman is jealous of another woman at some point. Female jealousy is rooted in fear, and specifically, a fear that she can be replaced. When a woman is no longer afraid that she can be replaced, she no longer is jealous. Now, no woman—I don't care how secure her husband tries to make her feel—is ever totally free of that fear in the natural. She must be freed in the spiritual first, and that means she must know who she is in Christ. She must come to know and believe in her spirit that she will *never* be replaced in God's love for her or in God's place for her on this earth. She must come to know her position in Christ—that it is secure, and that she is a designer's original, created as a one-of-a-kind woman. When a woman knows that God created her exactly as she is and begins to "work" with what God has given her to work with, then she moves out of fear and jealousy.

Not everyone was created to be a size 6. If you were created to be a size 22 . . . work it, baby!

Not everyone was given curly hair . . . or straight hair. No matter the texture of your hair as designed for you by God, work it!

Don't spend your time and energy fighting what God gave you to be your strengths! Don't let anyone make you but God. Don't let the world put you in its cookie-cutter mold. Don't become a factory-production model. If you give in to the way the world defines you, you will miss out on your unique qualities—the very qualities that make you valuable. What makes an antique or an artifact valuable? The fact that it is rare and distinct!

If God made you beautiful, use your beauty.

If God made you brainy, work your brain.

If God made you a computer genius, then work behind that computer to the glory of God.

If God made you a "natural" at business, then make a billion dollars and fund the expansion of the kingdom of God!

Whatever God has built into you, build on that, knowing that your position in Christ is secure and you don't ever need to be afraid that you will lose God's love.

Let me talk to you a little about fear.

Fear Is Based on What Appears to Be Real, but Isn't. Fear is based far more on what *isn't* than on what actually *is*. Fear—F-E-A-R—can stand for False Evidence Appearing Real.

It *appeared* to be a reality that Hannah's womb was shut up. She took the fact that she *hadn't* born children as "evidence" that she would *never* bear children. Her fear was built on false evidence that *appeared* real.

If you are going to defeat fear in your life, you must first identify what is real and what is imaginary. You must identify what you think is the truth of your situation and then ask yourself, "Does this line up with what God's Word says?"

Had God told Hannah that she would be barren? No.

Had God told Elkanah that Hannah would always be barren? No.

Was it God's desire that Hannah be blessed with children? Yes.

Children in that time were considered a sign of God's favor and reward. Had Hannah put herself in position to receive God's favor and reward? Yes.

If you are ever going to overcome fear in your life, you must face up to what it is that you are believing about yourself and your future and your relationship with God—and then see if what you are believing is in line with God's Word.

Are you saying about yourself what God says?

Are you anticipating a future that is what God has said belongs to you?

Are you in relationship with God according to what God has said and has promised?

Fear Is Incompatible with Love. God's Word says, "There is no fear in love; but perfect love casts out fear, because fear involves torment. But he who fears has not been made perfect in love" (1 John 4:18). Why is this so? Because love is total security. When you know that you are part of the Beloved and that God loves you with an infinite, unconditional, and unchanging love, you have a security inside you that no person can take away. You have a confidence that is rock solid. You have the kind of self-value and self-esteem that is godly because it is based on the way God values and esteems you.

If you live with constant jealousy and fear, you need to check your "love status." What is it that you aren't believing about God's love for you?

What hidden motives and desires and attitudes are you harboring inside you that are keeping you from experiencing God's love?

Love is incompatible with prejudice . . . and resentment . . . and anger . . . and bitterness . . . and unforgiveness. If you are harboring any of these attitudes or conditions in your life, you are not walking in love. And if you aren't walking in love, you are not secure. And if you aren't secure, you have opened your life up to fear.

Fear Is Fertilized by Words. You must stop listening to any word that fuels your fear. Cut those messages out of your life! Hannah could have said, "Peninnah, I'm not hearing you. Your provocations are falling on deaf ears." But she didn't. Hannah *listened* to what she should not have been listening to.

God's Word says, "Death and life are in the power of the tongue, and those who love it will eat its fruit" (Prov. 18:21).

Death includes destruction, ruin, and devastation. Life includes blessing, prosperity, and success. What you say—the tongue or language that you speak—will be what brings you destruction or success. It is what will set into motion the forces that result in your ruin or your blessing. Those that love what is said—in other words, those that give in to what is said and accept it and nurture it and hold it close to their hearts and nurse it and act on it—will eat the fruit or reward of their words.

Listen to what you are saying about yourself, even if it is just in your thinking. Who do you think you are? What labels are you putting on your life? How are you defining yourself?

Hannah may very well have told herself that she was barren so many times that it had become her identity—she no longer had any hope that she might not be barren all her life. And when a person loses hope, she weeps outwardly and inwardly. There's an overwhelming sadness that comes with the disappearance of hope.

Fear Builds over Time. Fear has a way of building up over time. In most cases the devil comes with a message of fear and discouragement a little bit at a time. He comes to wear you down until he wears you out. He comes to bring you to a place of exhaustion so that you lose your sense of pleasure and your enthusiasm for life. He wants to turn your joy into pain, your fun into fretting, your laughter into tears. Those kinds of changes in a person's emotional state don't happen overnight. They happen bit by bit by bit.

The enemy comes again and again and again. He comes to distract you from your source of strength—your praise and worship of the most high God. A little distraction, and a little distraction, and a little distraction.

If he hit you with a message of fear all at once, you'd see the enemy for who he is. If he hit you with a message of discouragement or distraction all at once, you'd understand that you aren't battling against flesh and blood but against principalities and powers, the rulers of darkness of this age, and spiritual hosts of wickedness in the heavenly places (see Ephesians 6:12).

The devil is subtle. He's crafty. He has devices that fly just under the radar of our spiritual awareness.

Peninnah knew how to "get to" Hannah. She knew just what messages to say day after day to eat away at Hannah's hope, her identity, her security. Hannah was jealous of Peninnah because Peninnah had children and she didn't. Can't you just see her pulling out the photograph album every day, pointing out all the fine qualities of her children and their progress through life? She knew which buttons to push. You'd better face up to the "buttons" in your life because I can assure you of this: the devil knows those buttons and he'll push them at any and every opportunity.

For her part, Peninnah was no doubt jealous of Hannah because Hannah had Elkanah's love. God's Word tells us, "Elkanah gave Hannah a double portion for he loved Hannah." Hannah received a double portion at the time of the offerings. She probably received a double portion in other material ways. Peninnah saw that double portion, and she knew that it meant Elkanah loved Hannah more than he loved her—it was a fact of life that was in her face every day and every night. Peninnah may have borne children to Elkanah, but Hannah had his heart.

The enemy is also jealous of your position with God. He doesn't want you in covenant relationship with God. He doesn't want you to be linked in a love relationship with God.

Peninnah wanted Hannah to lose her composure . . . her balance . . . her temper. She wanted Hannah to lose her position before Elkanah.

That's ultimately what the enemy wants in your life. He comes at you with messages that are aimed at your feelings of insecurity, jealousy, and other deep emotional needs to cause you to question your position before God. He comes again and again to instill doubt and fear in you, because a woman who knows her position in God is a *strong* woman with a *clear* destiny. The devil will do his utmost to keep you from birthing your destiny. His goal is to reduce you to despair and to tears.

TAKE THE PROBLEM TO GOD

The Bible says that Hannah became so upset that she "wept and did not eat." This once-a-year-feast was *supposed* to be the happiest day of the year. But Hannah wept.

Have you ever been there?

Have you stood at the altar and heard a man say, "till death do us part," only to have him leave you for a woman half your age?

Have you ever been betrayed by your best friend?

Have you ever had a child turn out to be something that you didn't make a mold for?

Have you ever felt that life had dealt you a hand that you didn't ask for or deserve?

The result can be that you become so broken . . . so devastated . . . so confused . . . and in so much pain . . . that you don't know where to turn or who to trust. When that moment comes . . . *turn to God!*

You must come to the point at which you recognize that no person can restore what is wrong inside you. No person can restore your hope. No husband can make it right. No child can solve the problem. No amount of money can "fix" it. No career can fill the void. Only God can do what needs to be done!

It's at that point that you will stop going to a person who is ultimately incapable of giving you what you know you need.

You'll no longer cling to your husband and demand that he give you the understanding he can't give.

You'll no longer cling to your job and demand that it give you the fulfillment you crave.

You'll no longer smother your children in your demand that they give you the feelings of value and worthiness you desperately want.

You'll no longer fight against a rival and demand that your rival give you the appreciation and love you desire.

You'll no longer demand something from a person who is totally incapable of giving it to you.

Many women don't understand why some people leave them— it might be a husband; it might be a boyfriend; it might be a friend. There are many reasons for a person to leave, but one of the main reasons is that some women set up demands, requiring things from their husbands and friends that no human being can give. No husband can meet all of a woman's needs. No friend can meet all of a person's needs. If a person feels that he is failing at providing what another person is desperate to receive and is demanding to receive, that person often just walks away. Don't demand from any person what only God can give you!

Only God can give you a deep awareness of how infinitely valuable and precious you are to Him, and what a glorious destiny He has for you.

Only God can see and meet the unmet needs in your life that even you don't recognize.

The good news in this jealousy war is that Hannah felt driven to God. She didn't turn on Peninnah. She didn't rage at Elkanah. She went to God.

There are some situations you must take to God and nobody else.

God's Word says to cast "all your care upon Him, for He cares for you" (1 Peter. 5:7). It doesn't say to cast all your cares on your pastor, on the committee, on your social club, on your boss, or on your best friend. There are cares that only God can take on His shoulders! There are cares only God can handle. There are bondages only God can break. There are situations only God can resolve. There are circumstances only God can change.

Only God can fix your heart.

Only God can mend your mind.

Only God could cause Hannah to conceive and bear a child.

Hannah's problem drove her to God.

DON'T LET ANYONE KEEP YOU FROM GOD

Don't waste your strength fighting your critic—go to God. Take action with God. And don't let anyone *keep* you from God.

At the entrance to the tabernacle of the Lord, Hannah poured out her heart. She was so deeply wounded that she wept there and prayed with her lips moving but without any sound coming from her mouth. She was misunderstood. The high priest, Eli, thought she was drunk.

Have you ever been misunderstood in your worship?

Have you ever been persecuted for your walk with God?

Have you ever been called names for taking a stand for Christ Jesus?

Have people ever made fun of you for going to church or giving your tithes and offerings or for clapping your hands and dancing as you praise God?

When Eli accused Hannah of being drunk, she didn't shrink away in silence. She spoke up. She said, "I'm not drunk, I'm a woman with a sorrowful spirit. I have poured out my soul before the Lord. I've been speaking out of the abundance of my complaint and grief" (see 1 Samuel 1:15–16).

Hannah was doing business with God, and nothing was going to deter her. This was not a typical sow-your-ten-dollars, pray-for-five-minutes, and say-a- "Praise-the-Lord-Amen" deal, which is the way many people seem to approach God with their deep needs. Hannah was looking for a breakthrough. Nothing else would do.

What we do in worship is not for the praise of men. We don't worship God in order to be popular with other people. What we do in worship is totally "unto the Lord." Even so, it hurts when people ridicule us and reject us.

Desperation drove Hannah to the Lord. And when you are desperate for a touch from God, the opinions of people won't deter you. When you are sick and tired of being sick and tired, you'll do whatever it takes to get your answer from God.

Are you desperate enough today to press toward God?

Is your pain producing perseverance in you?

Are you facing a need that is deep enough to drive you to push through any resistance that comes your way to get to God?

Some people today aren't desperate enough. They are content to live with their pain. They are willing to just "exist." God's Word says, "Because you are lukewarm, and neither cold nor hot, I will vomit you out of My mouth" (Rev. 3:16).

Stir yourself up today and press toward God!

PERSEVERE IN PRAYER UNTIL YOU GET YOUR ANSWER

Hannah refused to be denied. She said to Eli, "Do not consider your maidservant a wicked woman, for out of the abundance of my complaint and grief I have spoken until now" (1 Sam. 1:16).

And God spoke back to Hannah through the high priest. Eli said, "Go in peace, and the God of Israel grant your petition which you have asked of Him" (1 Sam. 1:17).

It's not enough for you to pour your heart out to God. You must persevere in pouring out your heart to Him until you get His answer back.

That answer may come as you read God's Word . . . as you hear a sermon on television, in church, or at a conference . . . or it may come from the still, small voice of God speaking in your heart. The answer may come into your mind and heart in a flash, or it may come to you slowly over time. But the answer will come. God's Word says:

- "Call upon Me in the day of trouble; I will deliver you, and you shall glorify Me" (Ps. 50:15).

- "The LORD is near to all who call upon Him (Ps. 145:18).

- "Call to Me, and I will answer you, and show you great and mighty things, which you do not know" (Jer. 33:3).

- "The same Lord over all is rich to all who call upon Him. For 'whoever calls on the name of the LORD shall be saved'" (Rom. 10:12–13).

God hears and God answers. When you call upon Him from the depths of your heart, He *will* answer you. And, He'll answer you in a way that will make you *know* it is His answer. What He says will happen, *will* happen.

Hannah's prayer of desperation was a prayer of faith. She looked to God to do for her what no person could do. She trusted God to hear and answer her, even if everybody around her misunderstood her. She had faith in God. Jesus said, "Have faith in God. For assuredly, I say to you, whoever says to this mountain, 'Be removed and be cast into the sea,' and does not doubt in his heart, but believes that those things he says will be done, he will have whatever he says. Therefore I say to you, whatever things you ask when you pray, believe that you receive them, and you will have them" (Mark 11:22–24).

God's Word says that faith has the power to give "life to the dead and calls those things which do not exist as though they did" (Rom. 4:17). Faith causes you to walk in the spirit realm and to put your belief in what God can do, is doing, and will do rather than on what you see around you. The only way you can have that kind of faith is to rest in God and trust in God no matter what, no matter what, no matter what.

It's saying . . .

I trust You to give me a baby, even if I'm ninety years old.

I trust You to provide for me, even if my cupboard is bare.

I trust You to let me see you face-to-face one day.

I trust You to deliver my children and to cause my children

to possess the gates of the enemy and to walk before You and serve You.

I trust You that my husband will rise up and call me blessed.

I trust You that no weapon formed against me will prosper.

I trust You that a thousand will fall at my side and ten thousand at my right hand.

I trust You that I can do all things through Christ Jesus.

God's Word says:

- "Let us hold fast the confession of our hope without wavering, for He who promised is faithful" (Heb. 10:23).

- "Do not cast away your confidence, which has great reward" (Heb. 10:35).

- "Without faith it is impossible to please Him, for he who comes to God must believe that He is, and that He is a rewarder of those who diligently seek Him" (Heb. 11:6).

I trust You.

I trust You.

I trust You!

WALK IN ASSURANCE . . . AND WORK YOUR STUFF!

Hannah did something about her situation. She went to the tabernacle and prayed—she sought God with her faith. And once she had given it over to God, she got up, wiped her tears, left her yesterday behind her, and began to walk in trust.

When faith graduates, it becomes trust. Trust is an assurance that God will do what God has said He will do. Trust is the assurance that God will be who God said He is, that He will fulfill what He has promised, and that He will accomplish what He has purposed.

There's a time to pour out your heart before the Lord and state your case with weeping and deep anguish of grief. There's a time to plead your case before God.

There's also a time to get up, wipe your tears, and walk away with trust—with confidence that God has heard you and will answer you.

There's a time to walk in your faith and say, "I believe it is so," even before there's any manifestation.

Hannah didn't just sit back and wait to see what would happen. No! She took action. She began to walk in trust. She wiped her tears, went back to the table, and ate. God's Word says, "Her face was no longer sad." She put a smile of joy and anticipation on her face. She had a knowing deep inside her . . . *God is at work. God is at work. God is at work. I don't know how. I don't know when. I don't know all the details, but God is at work. God is at work.* That's trust at work. That's what it means to trust—it means to walk forward in your life as if you are moving into position to receive the very thing God has promised.

Nothing about Hannah's situation had changed . . . but everything about Hannah had changed. Her attitude had changed. Her countenance changed. And she determined within herself that she would do what she could do, so that God could do what He could do!

The very next thing that the Bible tells us (King James Version) is that Hannah went home and she "knew" Elkanah. That word *knew* in the Hebrew means she took a bath, put on her best perfume and finest negligee, and made sure that Elkanah wasn't too tired that night. She had sexual relations with Elkanah. There was no way that Hannah was going to get pregnant if she didn't "know" Elkanah. She worked her stuff—she did her part!

146

I don't know what you're trusting God for today, but there's a part that you have to do. You have to put sneakers to your faith and walk out what you're believing God to do!

If you are believing God for a business, start working! Get a business plan. Find a piece of property. Start advertising. Get a loan if you need to. Find out how to make the business work.

If you are believing God for a ministry, start working! Preach to the shower tiles if that's the only place you have to preach. Preach to your cat and dog. Preach to the two-year-olds, and then to the four-year-olds.

Whatever you are believing God to do . . . start working at it!

Hannah "knew" Elkanah and she conceived Samuel. His name means "God hears." Hannah said she gave her son that name "because I have asked for him from the LORD" (1 Sam. 1:20).

When you start praying and give it all over to God—asking Him with all your heart for your heart's desire . . .

When you start walking in faith, with total assurance that God has heard you and will answer you . . . when you start putting action and works to your faith . . . you will start conceiving. The dream you have will be established in you. It will grow in you until the time God has for that dream to be delivered into this world, where it can produce a harvest that will lead to the expansion of His kingdom.

Are you provoked in your spirit today?

Are you at the point of weeping in anguish because of the bitterness of your soul?

Deal with it!

Go to God and pour out your grief and sorrow to Him. Get His word back to you.

And then get up and walk out that word. God has a dream for you to conceive today. Now is the time.

⌒ GOD'S WORD ON MARY MAGDALENE

Mary Magdalene lived in a city on the shores of the Lake of Galilee in Jesus' time. She had a face-to-face encounter with Jesus that changed her life. The Bible tells us that Jesus cast seven evil, demonic spirits from her life (see Mark 16:9). After being set free from these spirits that had ruled and ruined her life, she became a devoted and faithful follower of Jesus and was counted among a small group of women who, at their own expense, served Jesus and His disciples as they preached and ministered to the masses. The Scripture references about Mary Magdalene are John 20:1–3 and 10–14. They are found in the Appendix to this book.

7

MARY MAGDALENE

"My name is mud and it always will be."

Most theologians agree that Mary was a woman with a tainted past. She had a "reputation"—she was not the kind of woman a respectable man would have wanted to take home to meet Mama. She was known as a sinner.

Mary was from Magdala, a city on the southwest coast of the Sea of Galilee. This particular city had a reputation for being a city of prostitution.

Now, that does not mean that Mary was a prostitute. We don't know if she sold her body, but we do know that she was raised in a less-than-desirable environment. And we know that the atmosphere in which we are raised has an impact on our hearts—our intellect, our emotions, the intertwining of our souls and spirits. God's Word tells us that the issues of life flow from the heart (see Proverbs 4:23). What we see and hear and are constantly reminded of becomes ingrained in our spirits and souls. Mary was raised in an environment in which she very likely saw and heard and became familiar with things that affected her in a negative way.

What we *are* told about Mary Magdalene is that she was a woman "out of whom He had cast seven demons" (Mark 16:9). Can you imagine the mess a woman would be in with seven demons in her?

People are in a mess today without even one demon! They are

fooling around with Johnny . . . or Jamie. They are sleeping with Carlos . . . or Carolyn. They are using drugs with Freaky Freddie . . . or Freaky Freda. They are teaching Sunday school while they are filled with hatred and gossip. They are walking into church acting like Saint Susie or Saint Tyrone after a night of downing Jack Daniels and dancing with the devil.

Can you imagine the depravity, and then the despair, that must have filled Mary Magdalene?

The apostle Paul exposes the truth in 1 Corinthians 6:9–11:

> Do you not know that the unrighteous will not inherit the kingdom of God? Do not be deceived. Neither fornicators, nor idolaters, nor adulterers, nor homosexuals, nor sodomites, nor thieves, nor covetous, nor drunkards, nor revilers, nor extortioners will inherit the kingdom of God. *And such were some of you.* But you were washed, but you were sanctified, but you were justified in the name of the Lord Jesus and by the Spirit of our God.

Paul would say the same thing to us today: Such were some of you. Such *are* some of us.

And just because you haven't committed the sins Paul exposed, that doesn't mean you haven't *thought* about committing those sins or that you wouldn't have committed them if you had found yourself in the wrong atmosphere or environment. The fact that you didn't commit those sins is because Jesus got to you before you committed the sins. He rescued you!

God's Word tells us:

> Therefore, if anyone is in Christ, he is a new creation; old things have passed away; behold all things have become new.

Now all things are of God, who has reconciled us to Himself through Jesus Christ, and has given us the ministry of recon- ciliation, that is, that God was in Christ reconciling the world to Himself, not imputing their trespasses to them, and has committed to us the word of reconciliation. Now, then, we are ambassadors for Christ." (2 Cor. 5:17–20)

The word *in* when referring to being "in Christ" is a Greek word that denotes position—a relationship of rest. The only way you can ever overcome your condition is by knowing your position. Knowing "church" doesn't change you. Knowing a little bit of Hebrew and Greek doesn't change you. Knowing Christ and your position in Him changes you. When you know who He is, then you can know who you are in Him.

You are not of this world . . . you are *in Christ.*

To be a "new creation" in Christ means to be recently made, unused, fresh, and unprecedented. The old has passed away. There is a new way for you to look, to talk, to walk, to act, to respond to life.

God does not determine your future by the past experiences of your life. He sees the "end" of you—He sees down the line into your future and sees you transformed. He sees good things developing in you and good things coming to you and good things happening through you. God never binds you to your past—He frees you for your future.

God always speaks to us from our *future* states. When God came to a man named Gideon, he said to him, "The LORD is with you, you mighty man of valor!" (Judg. 6:12). Gideon said, "Who, me?" The Lord saw who Gideon was to be, not who he was.

God looks at you and calls you by what you *will* be. He calls you "anointed prophetess," "saint," "highly favored," "great soul winner," "world evangelist." We are so conditioned by looking at our situations that we forget God is way ahead of us and is talking to us from where we *will* be.

PEELING OFF THE LABELS OF LIFE

Mary was a woman who had been labeled by life.

Has a label been put on your life?

Poor?

Abused?

Sick?

Labels are put on the lives of people all the time, even those who are saved.

I know what it means to have a label slapped on your life.

For years Randy and I have worked in the inner city. One of our many projects is to gather together donations of school supplies, like new backpacks and shoes, and distribute them to inner-city children. Our desire is that children go to school with hope, dignity, and a reason to smile. It's one thing to be poor, as a fact. It's another thing to feel poor. We do not want children to feel poor. That is not the truth of God for their lives.

We teach inner-city children how to stand up straight. We teach them how to take care of the shoes on their feet and to wear their clothes with pride. We teach them to accept the dignity and value that God has placed on them. We teach them that what is inside of them is far greater than the environment that they live in.

The Word of God is higher than any natural or man-made law. It tells you who you are, what you can do, and what you can have.

If the Word of God says it . . . I can have it.

If the Word of God says it . . . I can be it.

If the Word of God says it . . . I can do it.

And so can you!

THE ABC'S FOR CONFRONTING LIFE'S LABELS

Years ago I learned the ABC's for confronting life's labels:

A *Stands for "Activator."* Identify the experience, conversation, or situation that "activated" the label in your life. A woman doesn't just wake up one day with the belief that she can't stand the way she looks or the life she lives. She usually has had that opinion for some time, through a number of defining moments, most of which may be from childhood. It's important that you ask yourself, When was this negative label first attached to my life . . . and by whom?

For many years, I thought I was ugly no matter what anybody else said to me. We all know the saying, "Sticks and stones can break my bones, but words will never hurt us." That saying is a lie! God's Word tells us the truth: "Death and life are in the power of the tongue" (Prov. 18:21). Words can wound far more than sticks and stones. Words can mark a young child's life in an indelible way.

If you believe the labels and lies that are put on you by people, rather than what the Word of God says about you, you will not have the power necessary to live a successful life.

I grew up firmly convinced that I was ugly, and therefore I spent years trying to win the approval of other people.

After I was saved, God put me in a two-year training program to learn the Word of God. One of the first things the Lord said to me was, "Paula, thank Me for your hands."

Now, my mother had said to me that my hands were beautiful— she called them "piano-player hands." They were like my daddy's hands. I began to praise God. "Thank You for my pretty hands. Thank You for my long and slender fingers."

And then God spoke in my heart, "Thank Me for your wrists." I said, "Lord, thank You for my beautiful wrists."

God said, "Thank Me for your forearms" . . . and then my

elbows. I used to joke as I looked in the mirror, "God, these elbows are so sexy they'll make a man lust!" In my heart, however, I truly became thankful to God for my elbows.

God didn't stop there, of course. He took me body part by body part over my entire body. I began to thank God for all of the physical me. I became aware as I had never been aware before that I am not just the product of the union between a man and woman. I am a creation of God! The Bible tells us, "We are His workmanship, created in Christ Jesus for good works, which God prepared beforehand that we should walk in them" (Eph. 2:10).

I realized that God had precisely, perfectly put me together. He chose the gene pool for my being. He chose the chromosomes that would be dominant in my body. He chose my ethnicity, my personality, my talents and abilities. I was conceived by a woman and a man, but I was designed by God!

I began to see my life through God's eyes.

The Bible tells us that we are "fearfully and wonderfully made" (Ps. 139:14). The word *fearfully* means "reverently."

To be "wonderfully" made means to be distinctively and uniquely created.

Many women today don't value themselves because they are looking to other people to set the standards for their lives. They are living by comparison—looking to people around them or to models in magazines to tell them what they *should* be, and by comparison, pointing out to them what they *aren't*. The truth of God is that you are a designer original! In fact, you are *the* Designer's original *you*.

You are not a cheap imitation of someone else. You are not a copy. You have your own specific physical identity—your own fingerprints and voiceprint and footprints and genetic code.

Embrace your distinctiveness! That's where you'll find your value.

When I was a child, my peers and even some of my teachers nicknamed me "MM." It stood for motormouth. One of my teachers pulled me aside one day and said, "You could really make something of your life if you just didn't run your mouth so much." Imagine!

God called me to preach with that motor mouth! He is the One who gave me a fluency of speech and ideas and an ability to speak in a powerful way to convey His powerful truths. Very often what other people see as your faults or foibles are the very things that God sees as your foremost assets waiting to be redeemed, strengthened, and fashioned in such a way that they bring glory to Him.

Take a look at what you are criticizing about yourself and what others seem to "hate" about you. Those very traits may very well be the ones that God is seeking to use for His purposes. God knew who He was creating when He created you!

Choose only the labels that God puts on your life. Activate what He says—and *only* what He says.

B *Stands for "Belief."* What label are you believing with such intensity that it has become your dominant thought?

Behavioral scientists tell us that a negative thought attached with a feeling can be repeated in a person's mind as many as six hundred times a day! It becomes what is called a *dominant thought.* And dominant thoughts drive behavior. They end up driving your entire life.

Are your dominant thoughts coming from God's Word or man's opinion?

When you know who you are, you develop a very solid self-esteem. You *believe* in yourself because you believe in what God says you are, are capable of doing, and can have.

Part of coming to that belief is recognizing that the Word of God applies directly to *you.*

It's reading Genesis 1:27 and saying, "So God created man in his own image, in the image of God created he him; male and female created he them."

It's reading James 1:17 and saying, "Every good gift and perfect gift is from above, and cometh down from the father of lights, with whom is no variableness, neither shadow of turning."

It's reading Romans 8:28 and saying, "All things are working together for *my* good because I am loved by God and called according to His purpose."

It's reading Psalm 35:27 and saying, "God's desire for *me* is that I prosper in all things, He takes pleasure in my prosperity."

Do you see yourself as gifted?

Do you see yourself as beautiful?

Do you see yourself as capable?

Do you see yourself as talented?

Do you see yourself as smart?

Let me remind you of two things that the enemy will also come to tell you anytime you have a dominant thought that isn't based on God's Word:

- *You are the only one in the world with this problem.* The enemy tries to isolate you. And when we buy into that lie, we *feel* isolated and lonely. Isolation and loneliness always are accompanied by frustration because we are creatures who were made for fellowship, love, and relationship—not isolation.

God's truth is that you are not alone. God is with you 24-7. He never leaves you nor forsakes you. God's Word says:

Fear not, for I am with you;
Be not dismayed, for I am your God.
I will strengthen you,
Yes, I will help you,
I will uphold you with My righteous right hand. (Isa. 41:10)

Jesus said to His followers, "I am with you always, even to the end of the age" (Matt. 28:20).

- *You will* always *have this problem.* The enemy will tell you that your situation cannot be resolved, settled, or cured. He tells you that what you have is incurable or unchangeable. When we buy into that lie, we feel despair. Hope and joy are drained out of us. And when hope and joy are drained from our lives, depression fills that void.

God's truth is that *all* things are possible with God. Absolutely *nothing* is impossible.

Both my grandmother and my great-grandmother suffered from depression. So did I in earlier years. One day, I decided that I was going to live in God's Word that says, "The joy of the Lord is my strength" (Neh. 8:10). I chose to be a joyful person! I said to my tendency to feel depressed, "I will not have depression. I will live in the joy of the Lord!" I chose to change my mind. You can change your mind as well. Do not allow any negative thought that would derail your destiny, to dominate in your thought life.

C *Stands for "Consequences."* How have you reacted emotionally and behaviorally since that label became stuck on you? What are the behaviors and habits that have resulted from your dominant thoughts and beliefs?

When a person has a renewed mind, beliefs change, and then subsequent behaviors change. At times, the renewal begins first in behavior. When a person begins to adopt new behaviors and habits based on God's Word, the new habits create a new character, and a new character creates a new destiny. Habits can drive beliefs.

Either way, it's ultimately up to you to *choose* to change your behavior, and that includes changing the environment and the atmosphere of your life. It includes changing your associations.

That's certainly the case with Mary Magdalene. She refused to reinforce the labels life had placed on her by remaining in the environment and in the relationships that first attached those labels to her. She changed her environment and her associations.

God's Word tells us that this woman with a tainted past was so transformed that she began to have companionship with Salome, the mother of James and John (John 15:40). She began hanging out with Mary, the mother of Jesus (John 19:25). She became close to Joanna, the wife of Chuza, who was King Herod's steward (Luke 8:2–3; 24:10). She became a woman of influence, associating with influential women.

Don't miss what God did! She went from night to day. She went from walking the streets to walking with Jesus. She went from bondage to freedom. She went from oppression and depression to joy and fulfillment. She went from being filled with evil to being filled with peace, prosperity, and love.

Mary Magdalene was not only *changed* from her past, but she was given the hope and promise for the future. She was transformed for her future.

Mary Magdalene was not a play-at-church, read-a-little-of-the-Word, double-minded woman. She was deeply committed to God. How do I know that? Because she became a giver. Those who worship God with all their hearts give to God. Those who aren't deeply committed to God don't give. Mary Magdalene gave of her substance to Jesus (Luke 8:2–3).

But then . . .

But then . . .

But then . . .

Oh, in so many of us today there is a "but then." God's Word tells us that *after* Mary Magdalene had been healed of evil spirits and infirmities . . . *after* she had provided for Jesus and His disciples from her substance . . . *after* she had experienced the newness of life that came from following Jesus and being in close association with Him . . . *after* all that, Mary Magdalene found herself at the tomb of Jesus, and it looked as if everything she had believed in had died. It looked as if the promise and dream that had filled her heart was over.

DON'T LET THE DEVIL STEAL YOUR PROMISE

Something inside Mary had died. Something had made her give up, to lose hope, to stop believing. She was at the point many women are at today—they have lost their promises and their dreams, and they can't seem to get them back.

Mary was a woman who needed to find her miracle once again in the midst of a mess.

Here is a woman who stands at the tomb and says of her Lord, "I don't know where they have taken Him."

She must have been thinking, *I don't know which is worse—to never have hope, or to have hope and then seemingly watch it disappear.*

Mary said, *"They* have taken away my Lord."

They can come in a lot of different packages. I don't know who *they* might be in your life.

I don't know who caused you so much confusion and pain.

I don't know who lied to you about who you are.

I don't know what made you abort what God promised you or what paralyzed you to keep you from acting on what you knew to be true.

But I do know this: the source behind "they" is the devil. Don't waste your strength fighting the wrong opposition.

God's Word tells us, "We do not wrestle against flesh and blood, but against principalities, against powers, against the rulers of the darkness of this age, against spiritual hosts of wickedness in the heavenly places" (Eph. 6:12). The devil will send all kinds of packages to take the Word away from you, because the Word is your destiny, and the devil will do his utmost to keep your destiny from being fulfilled.

If the devil can defeat the dream and destiny God has placed in you . . . if he can defeat the revelation of the Word inside you . . . then he can keep the harvest of that dream from happening.

Jesus taught:

Behold, a sower went out to sow. And it happened, as he sowed, that some seed fell by the wayside; and the birds of the air came and devoured it. Some fell on stony ground, where it did not have much earth; and immediately it sprang up because it had no depth of earth. But when the sun was up it was scorched, and because it had no root it withered away. (Mark 4:3–6)

When Jesus' disciples asked Him to explain this parable, here's what Jesus said:

The sower sows the word. And these are the ones by the wayside where the word is sown. When they hear, Satan comes immediately and takes away the word that was sown in their hearts. These likewise are the ones sown on stony ground who, when they hear the word, immediately receive it with gladness; and they have no root in themselves, and so endure only for a time. Afterward, when tribulation or persecution arises for the word's sake, immediately they stumble. (Mark 4:14–17)

The first thing the devil will do *immediately* is bring doubt and confusion to your mind. Doubt and confusion are his first weapons in trying to keep your dream from producing a harvest.

The second thing the devil will bring your way is a circumstance that will discourage you. If you don't fight against that discouragement, you will stop speaking the Word, meditating on the Word, and acting on the Word. You'll stop going deeper in the Word. You'll stop putting down roots in the Word that ground you and cause you to keep believing that, *no matter what happens,* what God has spoken to you *will* come to pass in your life. Those circumstances come in many packages. The devil will cause that spouse to walk out on you . . . that tragedy to happen to you . . . that disease to come upon you . . . that hard time to hit you. The devil will bring circumstances that leave you saying, "It isn't fair. It isn't right. God isn't faithful." The devil is a liar!

Jesus says that he comes with his lies and his discouraging circumstances—he comes with his "tribulation or persecution"—for the *word's sake* (Mark 4:17). The devil doesn't want to see any harvest from your life!

God has something ahead for you.

You must not let His dream die in you!

Paul wrote to the Philippians that he was "confident in this very thing"—this one thing, this one truth—that "He who has begun a good work in you *will* complete it until the day of Jesus Christ" (1:6, emphasis mine).

You don't need to know everything. You may never know much of anything. But make sure you know *this one thing:* Be confident that the God who started that good work in your life, that same God who gave you your dream, who rescued you out of the hellhole you were in, who cleaned up your messed-up life, who transformed you and made you a new creation, this same God *will* complete what He has started in you. To "complete" is to further execute and accomplish.

When you commit your ways to the Lord, He speaks all of His promises into your life. That Word of the Lord breathed into you causes something to happen. It causes something new to be birthed in you . . . and brought to the bud stage . . . and brought to the harvest stage of producing "seed" or "grain" . . . and brought to the fulfillment stage in which that grain is turned into "bread" that nourishes and satisfies your deepest desires. His Word once sent does not return void. It *accomplishes* what God sends it to do. It brings to wholeness the person to whom it is sent.

As you replace life's lies with God's Word, that Word of God becomes alive in your mind and heart. It becomes the seed that brings forth and buds. And the end result is that your former life—with all its guilt, sin, shame, failures, and labels—begins to pale in comparison to the wonderful glory of the new life God produces in you.

Stop looking back! God is pulling you to what's ahead! God's Word tells us about a man who said to Jesus, "Lord, I will follow You, but let me first go and bid them farewell who are at my house." But Jesus said to him, "No one, having put his hand to the plow, and looking back, is fit for the kingdom of God" (see Luke 9:61–62). This man wasn't backsliding or returning to a past life for one more good ol' time. This man just wanted to go *back* to old associations. Jesus said, "If you're looking back, you're unfit to move forward." That word *unfit* means unsuitable, improper, unqualified. The kingdom is the rule, realm, and reign of God. Looking back isn't what makes you qualified to rule and reign in the kingdom of God! If you are living in yesterday, you will not be ready for tomorrow.

Yesterday is in the tomb. Today is in the womb. And what you are pregnant with right now is what you will bear in the future!

Instead of focusing on what should have been, would have been, might have been, or was . . . focus on what God says *will* be. What you focus on is what you will master. What you look at longest becomes strongest in your life. If something captures your attention and you are meditating on it, you will eventually act on it. What you focus on becomes what you *do*.

The Lord spoke to Joshua, "This Book of the Law shall not depart from your mouth, but you shall meditate on it day and night, that you may observe to do according to all that is written in it. For then you will make your way prosperous, and then you will have good success" (Josh. 1:8). To meditate is to "see" what God sees, to "see" yourself doing what God says you can do, and to "see" yourself possessing what God says you can possess. If you continue to speak God's Word and see your life through the lens of what God says you are and will be, you will act in a way that brings God's blessings to pass in your life. If you will do these three things—speak the Word, meditate on the Word, and act on the Word—*then* you will have prosperity and success.

If you lose your focus—if you stop speaking the Word and meditating on it and acting on it—you will become distracted, and soon you will begin to wonder if it really was God who spoke in your heart to write that book or produce that record or start that business or teach that class. The enemy comes to abort the dream with which God impregnated you. He comes to keep the treasure in you sealed up.

God's Word says, "We have this treasure in earthen vessels, that the excellence of the power may be of God and not of us" (2 Cor. 4:7). What God has put in you is *treasure*. That word in the Greek means a deposit of wealth . . . of value. Treasure is what God has given you as your gifts and talents. It is the Spirit that God has placed in you.

Why do you have this treasure? That the "excellence of the power of God" might be manifested in your life.

You are not a product of what has happened to you or what other people have said about you. You are the product of what is in you and *who* is in you to produce "excellence of power."

Mary Magdalene said, "I do not know where they have laid

Him." The Bible says that she then turned around and saw Jesus standing there, but she did not know that it was Jesus. She could not perceive that He was alive. Her promise, her dream, her hope was standing right in front of her, but she could not perceive it, she could not "see" with her faith, and she could not "believe" it was so.

Mary Magdalene couldn't get her eyes off the problem—the empty tomb, the not knowing where Jesus was. And because she couldn't get her eyes off the problem, she couldn't see the Problem Solver. Because she couldn't get her eyes off what had died, she couldn't see the power of the resurrected Christ standing right in front of her.

Open your spiritual eyes! See that God is working on your behalf. See that God is causing your seed to grow and that a harvest is coming. See that God is preparing you for the destiny that is still to come.

I don't know what dream you had from God. But I do know this: He never intended for it to die forever. He intends for that dream to live and produce a harvest that will extend on until eternity. He intends for that dream and that destiny to be fulfilled in you.

What is your dream?

What is it that you once were so passionate about?

What is it that you once fasted and prayed for?

Has that dream died? What precisely has "died" on the inside of you?

Deal with it!

Today is the day to regain your focus. Put your eyes on the future God has for you.

Today is the day to start to replace all of life's lies and labels with God's truth.

Today is the day to speak the Word, meditate on the Word, and act on the Word.

Today is the day to look again at the talents and gifts God has placed in you. Today is the day for that dream to be resurrected!

Today is the day to rise up and begin to birth the dream that God put in your heart.

Stop weeping and see the Resurrection standing before you! Put your trust in Him and reclaim the promise He placed in your heart.

～ GOD'S WORD ON THE SHUNAMMITE WOMAN

This notable woman of Shunem, whose name we are not given, lived in the time of the great prophet Elisha. She went beyond the normal protocol of hospitality and created a room especially for Elisha so he might stay at her home anytime he was passing her way. Elisha, in return, spoke the Word of God into her life to give her the one thing she desired but did not have: a son. The Scripture references on the Shunammite woman are 2 Kings 4:8–10 and 4:14–17, and they are found in the Appendix to this book.

8

THE SHUNAMMITE WOMAN

"Freaky Freddie isn't coming through for me."

The Shunammite was a woman who knew how to capture the moment. She knew how to seize the opportunity. She didn't let a great man of God pass her by without constraining—insisting and persuading—him to stop and eat at her home. God's Word tells us that she was a noble woman, a "great" woman. She had an inner awareness that Elisha was a "great" prophet. And she didn't let a great prophet pass her by.

There's something we must recognize about great prophets of God. Great prophets walk along great paths. They walk according to a great plan and purpose. They know that life is not chaotic—they know their lives are *planned* by God. They know that God has a purpose for them and for every person. They know God has a *destiny* for every person.

In insisting that Elisha, the great prophet, stop and eat at her home, this woman of Shunem was inserting herself into the path of this great flow of God's plan and purpose that was at work in Elisha's life. In doing that, she was claiming a destiny of God for her own life. And she didn't stop with just one meal. She fed him many meals. She had a room prepared at her home so that *every* time Elisha passed her way, he would feel free to stop and spend the night at her house. She created an atmosphere inviting the presence and purpose of God into her life.

She was a great woman . . . but she wanted the greatness of Elisha present in her life so that she could become an even *greater* woman of faith and destiny.

How does a person become great?

God often breeds greatness out of the worst situations a person can ever imagine. Trouble is an incubator for greatness. God's Word says, "God is our refuge and strength, a very present help in trouble" (Ps. 46:1). His strength more than matches our trouble. Every person who is ever born in a natural way is born under pressure—the pressure of labor pains *push* us into life. We are pushed into a more powerful position. We are pushed toward our destiny. There's a resistance and a pushing for everything good that produces life. That's true in the natural. It's true in the spiritual.

The Lord knew exactly the pressure you needed to get you to the place you are. He knows the pressure it will take for you to birth what He has for you in your future. God's Word says, "The Lord knows how to deliver the godly out of temptations" (2 Peter 2:9). He knows *exactly* what forces need to come against you and how to deliver you from them, so that by your coming up against those forces and experiencing God's delivering power, you are strengthened for what lies ahead. It is the pressure you have experienced that pushes you into God's power.

I don't know what situations this woman from Shunem had experienced, but I do know that she hadn't arrived at a position of being a notable or "great" woman without having gone through some things. God had prepared her for the moment when the prophet of God would walk by her door. And what's important for us to learn from her is that she didn't let that moment pass her by. She had a sovereign, God-ordained, and God-planned appointment with Elisha, even though she may not have known it at the time. She didn't miss her appointment.

God's Word also tells us that she recognized Elisha was a holy man. She called him a holy man. Holy means "separated" or "set apart" for God's purposes. She knew Elisha wasn't like every other man. She knew he had something to give to her that no other person could give . . . he had a role to play in her life . . . he had a function and a purpose that was godly.

So many people today miss the true role that their pastors or spiritual mentors have in their lives. They expect their pastors to be like a politician—to be a hand shaker and a baby kisser. They want them to show up with a smile at their weddings and a tear at their funerals. They expect them to become bondsmen for them—constantly bailing them out of trouble. The real function of a man of God, however, is to feed the flock of God. The role of your pastor is to give you a word from the Lord so that you will be nourished and built up with strength and power to fight against the enemy of your soul who comes against you to steal from you, destroy you, and kill you (see John 10:10).

The Shunammite knew in her heart that this holy man, Elisha, had a word for her. He had something to say to her that would change her life and empower her to walk into her destiny. She knew he had a faith worth following.

Oh, how important it is to find a person who is worth following! How important it is to make a *place* for that person in your life!

Elisha had a vision of her life that was worth seeing.

Elisha had a word for her life that was worth hearing.

Elisha had a purpose for her life that was worth pursuing.

Elisha had a faith that was worth following.

WHO ARE YOU FOLLOWING?

Who are you following today? Who have you chosen as your leader?

The truth is, we all follow somebody. None of us makes it

alone or on our own. We follow those who have gone before. We follow those who are more mature. We follow teachers and mentors and leaders. We follow preachers and pastors. We follow those who *lead*.

The truth of God is also that not every leader can or will take you where God wants you to go.

Not every self-proclaimed "leader" is right for *you*.

Not every person in a leadership role in your life is a good leader. Not every parent is a good parent worth emulating. Not every teacher is worth learning from.

Not every leader is worth following.

Let me share something important with you about the limitation of a spiritual leader, whether that person is a man or a woman. A person can lead you only as far as that person can "see" with his faith. He cannot enable you to "see" what he cannot "see" with his spiritual eyes.

A leader cannot believe for something in your life that he doesn't believe for his own life. He can't take you to a place he doesn't believe you can go.

Moses is a prime example of this. God's Word tells us that Moses was anointed and called to deliver the Israelites from the bondage of Egypt. But . . . Moses could not take the people *into* the promised land. He could take them into the wilderness—he'd been in the wilderness before. He had been in a wilderness for forty years before God called him to lead the Israelites out of Egypt and into a wilderness. He knew how to trust God and walk out into a wilderness.

Moses could lead the people across the Red Sea. He had been delivered out of a body of water in his own life when he was just a baby.

Moses could believe for God to provide for the people. He had experienced God's provision in the house of Pharaoh and later in the house of his father-in-law.

Moses could believe for God to perform powerful miracles of deliverance. He had seen the power of God at work in his own life— he had seen his rod turn into a snake, and then back into a rod. He had seen his hand turn leprous as white as snow, and then be restored fully to normal flesh. Moses could believe for water to be turned to blood and for plagues to start and be stopped.

Moses could not see, however, how God could take a murmuring, stiff-necked, hard-hearted people and transform them into a powerful army of faith to take the promised land. God showed him the land of promise. He took him to a high mountain and showed him the full length and breadth of the land. He said, "This is the land. I will give it to the Israelites. I have caused you to see it, but you shall not cross over there" (Deut. 34:4). Why not? Because Moses had acted in anger against the very people God was going to take into the promised land.

Moses could not lead where Moses could not "see" with faith to go.

Joshua was able to see more. Joshua had seen the people in battle because he had been in battle with them. Joshua had seen the new generation grow up in faith, gathering manna and treading out the land with shoes that didn't wear out. Most important of all, Joshua had been *in* the land of promise as one of the twelve spies—he had been one of only two who had said, "We can take this land because God has promised it to us" (see Numbers 13). Joshua could see the victory. He could lead the people into the conquest of the land because he could see what Moses could not see.

What is it you are seeing with your faith today?

Are you following a leader who helps you to see more than you can see? Are you following a leader who is helping you to hear more than you've heard about the power and greatness and provision and glory of God? Are you following someone who believes for more than you currently believe for? Are you following someone who can help you experience God in a way that's beyond what you've ever experienced?

Trust God to Send You His Leader. Trust God to send you the right leader to lead you into your destiny. Ultimately, you don't *find* God's leader for your life. God *sends* that leader your way. Your role is not to *find* your leader. Your role is to recognize the leader that God sends, invite that leader into your life, and choose to follow that leader.

The Shunammite did not *send* for Elisha. She did not seek him out. God sent him her way. She saw him and invited him in and made a place for him.

Now, to invite a leader into your life does not mean that you necessarily seek a face-to-face, one-on-one relationship with that person. It doesn't mean you develop an intimate friendship with the person. It means that you invite what the person says to penetrate your mind and to take up lodging in your heart and your soul. It means that you invite that person to "speak" into your life because you have open ears that are eager to hear what the person has to say.

You need to be looking with both eyes wide open for the leader God will send your way. It may be a person you see on television or hear on the radio. It may be a person you encounter at a conference or retreat. It may be a person who is speaking at your church next week. Be looking. God will send that person!

TAKE A LOOK AT YOUR ASSOCIATIONS— AND DO THE MATH!

There are four types of people in life:

> People who add to your life
> People who subtract from your life

People who multiply what God is doing in your life

People who divide you from your God-given purpose in life

We must make very certain that we are associating only with people who are adding and multiplying in our lives! If a person is subtracting or dividing, you need to separate yourself from that person.

Now, I will minister to *everyone*. Everyone qualifies for ministry. But I fellowship with very few. You need to audit your relationships—you need to make sure you have a balance between the withdrawals people make from your life and the deposits they make into your life. If you have too many people withdrawing ministry from you, and not enough people depositing into you the goodness of God, you will end up in the "red." You will end up depleted—bankrupt emotionally and exhausted physically. If you end up in the "red," you will never reach your destiny.

Everybody that passes your way isn't worth your attachment.

Lots of people passed through Shunem. The Shunammite only prepared a room for one of them—Elisha.

There are some people you need to let walk right on by your life. Don't invite them in. Don't make a place for them. Don't go out and walk the road they're on.

God's Word tells us, "Do not be deceived: 'Evil company corrupts good habits'" (1 Cor. 15:33). You become a product of who and what you are around. The Bible also says, "He who walks with wise men will be wise, but the companion of fools will be destroyed" (Prov. 13:20). If you attach yourself to wise people, you will become wise. If you hang around fools, you will become a fool. That's why you need to attach yourself to people who will assist you toward your destiny, not away from it.

Withdraw from Those God Tells You to Leave Behind. Don't take into your future the people God tells you to leave in your past. Don't continue in association with them. And don't harbor their memories in your soul. Let them go!

The first thing God said to Abram was, "Get out of your country, from your family and from your father's house, to a land that I will show you" (Gen. 12:1). Abram was 99.9 percent obedient . . . but he took his nephew into his future. He took Lot, "his brother's son," with him when he left Haran. There was nothing but heartache and headache in Abram's doing that.

You cannot drag your past into your future! You may be lonely for a few nights . . . you may not have anybody to hang out with for a few weekends . . . you may not have the phone ringing off the wall like you once did . . . but in the end, you'll be free to walk into your destiny, and God will have new friendships, new relationships, and new purposes for you that will far surpass the old.

Lot brought strife into Abram's life—he brought envy and a self-seeking spirit. He brought confusion. God's Word tells us that the land was not able to support the flocks and herds and tents of both Abram and Lot. The day came when "Abram said to Lot, 'Please let there be no strife between you and me, and between my herdsmen and your herdsmen; for we are brethren. Is not the whole land before you? Please separate from me. If you take the left, then I will go to the right; or, if you go to the right, then I will go to the left" (Gen. 13:8–9). There was an eventual separation of their ways. There had to be!

Those who have a spirit of strife will always gravitate toward evil. They are led by what they see—what they sense with their physical senses as being pleasurable. Lot chose the plain of Jordan and the cities of Sodom and Gomorrah. He chose a place that was filled with evil. He chose the plain of Jordan because it looked well-watered and green and lush "like the garden of the Lord." It *looked* good, but underneath, it was evil.

You need to get Lot out of your life! You need to let go of all those old associations that are creating strife and confusion.

Withdraw from Those Who Refuse Spiritual Authority. Jesus gave very clear instructions about this. He said, "If your brother sins against you, go and tell him his fault between you and him alone. If he hears you, you have gained your brother. But if he will not hear, take with you one or more, that 'by the mouth of two or three witnesses every word may be established.' And if he refuses to hear them, tell it to the church. But if he refuses even to hear the church, let him be to you like a heathen and a tax collector" (Matt. 18:15–17). The Jews in Jesus' day had *no* relationship with the heathen, who were the Gentiles, or with tax collectors.

Withdraw from those who have put themselves above or apart from spiritual authority. Have no fellowship with them!

"But," you may be saying, "I just want to minister to them."

The way you minister to them is to refrain from association with them until they come under spiritual authority.

Withdraw from Those Who Invite You to Sin. Withdraw from those who are in immoral and illegal and illicit relationships. The person who will sin *with* you is a person who eventually will sin *against* you. When you know to do better and you don't do it, it's counted as sin to you. And sin bears consequences. It steals, kills, or destroys something in you. It may be your innocence that is stolen. It may be your reputation that is destroyed. It may be your health that is damaged. It may be your emotional well-being that is injured. Sin will always kill your ability to trust that person completely or to respect that person fully.

If you steal *with* another person . . . that person will eventually steal from you.

If you gossip *with* another person . . . that person will eventually gossip about you.

If you enter into a relationship through adultery or fornication, until God fully transforms that person, you will be haunted by the fact that he or she will potentially sin against you someday.

Paul said, "You yourselves know how you ought to follow us." The truth of God is that we *do* know God's commands. We do have a sense of what is right and wrong. We do have a conscience. We do know who is doing what is moral, legal, and right . . . and who isn't. We do know!

We are to walk in what we know is right!

CONFRONT YOUR OWN "NEEDINESS"

"But I have needs," some people say. "I need my friends from my former life."

We all have needs. But the only need that we should seek to meet with all our hearts, minds, and souls is our need for God. Anything you need more than you need God is either an idol or an addiction in your life.

Take a look at your neediness. Take a look at the reason you think you *need* someone or something in your life. Take a look at the way you value yourself. Your need flows out of what you believe about yourself and what you think you deserve.

We always attract subconsciously what we *think* we deserve. That is the message of Numbers 13. The Israelites sent spies into the land of Canaan and they came back saying, "We are not able to go up against the people, for they are stronger than we . . . the land through which we have gone as spies is a land that devours its inhabitants, and all the people whom we saw in it are men of great stature. There we saw the giants (the descendants of Anak came from the giants); and we were like grasshoppers in our own sight, and so we were in their sight" (Num. 13:31–33). It was as the Israelites saw themselves that the Canaanites saw them—the Israelites saw themselves as "grasshoppers" and therefore, so did the Canaanites.

The problem was not the enemy. It wasn't the giants. It was the Israelites' self-perception that was the problem. It was the way they

failed to value themselves, the promises God had given to them, and the power of God to bring those promises to fulfillment.

We each send off silent signals all the time about the way we value ourselves. I don't have a problem with men trying to make a move on me or pick me up. I don't think it's because I'm unattractive . . . I simply send off signals that I am unavailable. I don't have a problem with men saying lewd or off-color things to me. I don't think its because I'm a poor listener . . . I simply send off signals that I'm not interested in hearing that kind of language. Men have egos and they don't go after something they don't think they can get. If a woman sends off signals that she's "off limits," men don't trespass on her life.

A woman sends off silent signals in the way she walks, the way she holds her head, the way she dresses, and the way she comes into a room. She sends off signals in the way she talks and in the way she looks people in the eye. The signals tell another person the way she values herself.

If men are always making a move on you, or if people are always telling you off-color jokes, take a look at the signals you are sending! Are you sending signals that say you are available, desperate, and needy? Or are you sending signals that say you are respectable and belong to God and are trusting Him to meet all your needs?

If you believe you are to be the "head and not the tail," then you will walk as the "head" (see Deuteronomy 28:13). If you believe you are to be "above only, and not be beneath," then you will act in ways that send the message, "I'm blessed by God."

The problem with some people is that they don't believe they can ever be more than a seven-dollar-an-hour employee. They don't believe they *can* be the owner of their own companies. Simply put, they don't realize the value that is within themselves. It's when a person begins to value himself that he develops himself.

"But I didn't get three doctorates," you may be saying.

No . . . and neither did Bill Gates, arguably the richest man in the world right now. He dropped out of college. But he never stopped valuing himself—he never stopped valuing his own brain and his own ingenuity and his own desire to succeed.

The problem with some people is that they don't believe they can ever have enough money to pay their bills. They don't believe they can have financial prosperity. Why? Because they don't believe they *deserve* to have money . . . and they don't respect the money they do have. They spend it in all sorts of crazy ways instead of investing it in things that have some lasting worth to them.

People tell me they want more friends . . . but they don't respect and value people who come their way who might become their friends.

People tell me they want more of God's anointing . . . but they don't respect the anointing they do have.

When you violate something good that God sends your way, God will not send you more of it! And the truth is, anything you don't value, you violate. And what you don't value in yourself, others will also violate.

Jesus said, "You shall love your neighbor as yourself" (Matt. 22:39). You can't really love another person unless you love yourself *first*. You won't value another person unless you value yourself first. And the opposite is also true—others won't love and value you unless you love and value yourself *first*. They will respond to you the way *you* respond to yourself.

When you love yourself, you attract other people to you who will value you for who you esteem yourself to be.

CHOOSE LEADERS WHO WILL CALL YOU TO A HIGHER PURPOSE AND A GREATER PROSPERITY

God's Word says, "Remember those who rule over you, who have spoken the word of God to you, whose faith follow, considering the outcome of their conduct" (Heb. 13:7). Keep your eyes on those who are godly examples. God has put them in your path to help you. Look at their lifestyle of faith. Look at their conduct. Believe as they believe. Act as they act. We are to follow leaders as they follow Christ. Now, don't misunderstand me and put a person on an unrealistic pedestal, for we are all merely human. No one is God but God alone. John the Baptist was a voice that cried in the wilderness to prepare the way of the Lord. He was "a voice," but he was not *the* Voice. His voice was to lead you to the "one whose shoes he was not worthy to lace" (Acts 13:25). It is the faith—the Word of God that is activated and operating within a person—that you are to follow. That faith should lead you into an intimate relationship with the Lord. It is through that relationship that you will find and fulfill your purpose and destiny.

Choose to follow leaders who have a higher purpose—those who are following Christ no matter what happens. Look for those who are faithful in good times and bad. Look for those who rise above their circumstances to pursue a higher calling on their lives.

Choose to follow leaders who experience prosperity. Prosperity is not just a matter of finances or material possessions. *Prosperity* is a wholeness word—it refers to your soul leading the way, and your body and material possessions coming into alignment with the health of your soul. God's Word says, "Beloved, I pray that you may prosper in all things and be in health, *just as your soul prospers*" (3 John 2).

Prosperity refers to the *whole* of life, not just one slice of it. Look for leaders who have been made whole by Christ Jesus and who are pursuing even greater wholeness day by day.

Paul said to all those whom he led to Christ, "Follow me as I follow Christ." We are to do the same today—choose to follow those who clearly are following Christ.

Don't follow people who are lazy or who would rather party than work. Proverbs says, "He who tills his land will have plenty of bread, but he who follows frivolity will have poverty enough!" (28:19). The word for *frivolity* in the King James Version is translated "vanity." The result of those who pursue frivolity is the opposite of prosperity—it is poverty. Poverty is more than being broke, busted, and disgusted. It is also a condition of the spirit—it is the opposite of prosperity. Poverty means you will be malnourished in your soul.

Don't follow vain people—they are empty people with empty goals. The Bible says, "Charm is deceitful and beauty is passing, but a woman who fears the LORD, she shall be praised" (Prov. 31:30). Vanity refers to the *superficial*—it's a word that refers to the outside more than the inside, to the temporary instead of the eternal, to the passing fad instead of the sure foundation. If you follow empty, vain people who have no substance to them, you will have no substance in yourself. You will not be able to succeed, nor will you be empowered for blessing.

Let me tell you five traits of vain people:

1. *Vain people are critical of those who prosper.* And again, I'm not referring to prosperity in financial terms. *Prosperity* in the Bible is a term that refers to the whole of a person's being. *Prosperity* is a word that speaks of success in every area of life. God's Word says, "God shows no partiality" (Acts 10:34). The book of Hebrews says, "Jesus Christ is the same yesterday, today, and forever" (Heb. 13:8). God has promised prosperity to those who are faithful in following God's commandments. They are the ones who have *souls* that prosper, and in like manner, their bodies, finances, minds, and relationships prosper as well.

We should rejoice when we see our brother or sister being blessed. If that person is blessed on Monday, you may be the one who is blessed on Tuesday. If God raised that person up in January, you may be the one who is raised up in February.

2. *Vain people are always looking at flaws.* There's a children's nursery rhyme that tells about a cat that found itself in the glory of the queen's

throne room, and all that cat could see was the mouse in the corner of the room. That's what vain people do. They miss out on the glory, splendor, and power of God because they are too busy looking at the sinner sitting across the aisle from them in church. Vain people are always looking for one little aspect of human failure, instead of seeing the bigger picture of what God is doing and what will be God's success.

There's always going to be a mouse in the room. There's always going to be something that detracts or distracts. Keep your focus on the glory and greatness of God.

What you look at longest will be what becomes strongest in your life. God's Word says, "Let your eyes look straight ahead, and your eyelids look right before you. Ponder the path of your feet, and let all your ways be established. Do not turn to the right or the left; remove your foot from evil" (Prov. 4:25–27). Don't allow yourself to get distracted from what God is doing. If you focus on flaws, you will become a critical person and you will miss the purpose and call of God.

3. *Vain people are complainers.* If you complain, you remain in the situation you don't like. Complaining is a trap. Complainers never rise above or move beyond those things that are the focus of their complaint. God calls us to be "praisers." When you praise, you raise. This is especially true in times of adversity. When you praise, you raise your eyes from the problem and to the Problem Solver. When you praise, you get your eyes off what *is* wrong and on the goal of what *can be* right. When you praise, you get your focus off the adversity and on the blessing that God has ahead for you.

Never forget that the degree of your adversity will be the degree of your success . . . if you will keep your praise and fuel your faith.

Everybody has struggles, bad days, trauma, and trouble. You need to get your eyes off the bad things that are trying to hold you down and get your eyes on the One who can lift you up! Believe God's Word that you can do all things through Christ who strengthens you! (see Philippians 4:13).

I once laid my hands on a woman who was told by doctors that she had no womb and no ovaries and no fallopian tubes . . . and a year later, I saw that woman holding twins.

I once prayed for a man who was hooked up to machines and had no brain wave and was declared "brain-dead" . . . and two weeks later, I watched that man praising God in church.

I have seen people who had HIV and AIDS, blind eyes, and inoperable brain tumors healed by the power of God. Don't tell me that God cannot heal your situation. Don't tell me that God cannot release you from the bondage you're in. Don't tell me that God cannot deliver you and make you whole. God can do all things! He is the God of the impossible. He is the God of the supernatural.

The facts may be disastrous, dire, and deadly.

The truth is *everything* the Word of God says. The truth is that we are in this world, but we are not *of* this world. The truth is that the Word of God is more powerful than anything on this earth. The truth is that the spoken Word of God does not return void—it has the power to heal, to resurrect, to deliver, to make whole, and to prosper. It has the power to create the very miracle you need!

If you complain, you remain. If you praise, you raise.

4. *Vain people act as if the world owes them something.* They have a victim mentality, which is a mentality that says, "I can't succeed unless you let me succeed" . . . "I can't get out unless you let me out" . . . "I can't do anything unless you allow me to do it."

Nobody should ever be given that kind of power over your life.

Nobody should ever be given that kind of control over your destiny.

The truth is, God does not want you to have a victim mind-set. He doesn't want you looking to the world or to people to make it possible for you to be blessed. He wants you to look to Him for all things!

His rules—not man's rules—are the rules that produce prosperity.

His commands—not man's commands—are the commands that produce life and blessing.

His principles—not man's principles—are the principles that produce wisdom and power.

God alone should be the One to whom you turn and say, "I surrender all." God alone should be the One to whom you say, "Not my will, but Your will be done."

5. *Vain people see the problem and not the solution.* If you follow a vain person, that person's empty goals will produce empty goals in you. You cannot get to success and prosperity if the goals you are aiming at are empty and futile. The end of vanity is poverty—a lack in every area of your life.

So many people today are wondering, "Why is there so much lack in my life? Why don't I have the power, protection, or provision of God?"

They need to take a long hard look at their relationships and associations. They need to see who and what they are following. And if they are following vain people—empty people with empty goals—they need to find someone else to follow!

Again, let me remind you of this truth: We *choose* those we will follow. We must also choose to see what they can see that is for our blessing and our destiny.

The Shunammite could not *see* how God could give her a child. But Elisha could see it.

The man who was brought to Jesus could not see. But his friends could see.

You may not be able to see today the future God has for you. But there are people whom God will call into your life who do have the ability to see your future. It may be a teacher . . . or a pastor . . . or a coach . . . or a spiritual counselor.

God's Word tells us that when the blind man was brought to Jesus, Jesus "put His hands on his eyes again and made him look up." Jesus had led him out of town and touched him once, and the man could see—but he saw men as trees walking. Jesus touched him again. The second time he could see "everyone clearly" (Mark 8:25).

Jesus repositioned this man. He took him out of town and away from those who had unbelief. Do you need to be repositioned today?

Jesus refocused this man's attention. He made him "look up." Do you need to have your attention refocused on the most high God?

Jesus touched him a second time. Do you need a second touch so you can see clearly the destiny God desires for you to birth?

God has an appointment of destiny for you. He comes to you to reveal His eternal call on your life. God then comes to you to reveal His destiny for you on this earth. He wants you to see your destiny clearly so that you will believe for it to come to pass.

Our problem is not that God has failed to provide a plan and purpose that is distinctly and uniquely ours. Our problem is that we have not yet *seen* all that God has for us. Our problem is that we have not continued to *believe* that what God has destined for us will come into reality.

Choose to follow leaders who will help you see *clearly* what God has for you.

THE ASSOCIATIONS WORTH DEVELOPING

There are four associations that are worth developing—in other words, there are four types of associations you need to welcome into your life and then develop with your time, energy, and resources.

1. *Choose to develop associations with people who focus on your future, not your past.* Choose to hang around people who don't see *where you are* nearly as much as they see *where you are going*.

Do the people in your life have the same purpose you have?

Do they have the same destiny?

When you look at another person, don't look at where that person is today. Look to what God has destined for that person and encourage the person to pursue his or her destiny.

2. *Choose to associate with people who see your potential as being unlimited.* Your only limitations are the limitations you place on yourself. You can be as "big" as you allow God to be "big" inside you!

If you believe God to heal a cold, He'll heal a cold. If you believe God to heal cancer, He'll heal cancer. If you believe God to raise the dead, He'll raise the dead.

If you believe God to save your family, He'll save your family. If you believe God to save your community, He'll save your community. If you believe God to shake nations, He'll shake nations.

Take the limitations off God! God will be as *big* as you allow Him to be.

That's why it is so important to see who you are in the Spirit. That's why it's so important to be around people who talk to you about your destined state and about developing your gift of God.

So many people try to hold others back or control others or keep other people down. They are insecure and jealous. They don't want others to succeed because they believe that if others succeed, they will be "lesser" in some way. The truth of God is that we must help and encourage others to succeed.

Don't let your gender as a woman hold you back.

Don't let your marital state hold you back.

Don't let your age hold you back—you are never too old or too young to be used by God.

Don't let your background hold you back.

Abram was a "heathen" man when God spoke to him. He was called out of a heathen land. But Abram believed God and God said, "Look up at the stars. Try to count them. The number of stars you can count is the number of descendants you will have one day." As much as you can see with your spiritual eyes, that's how much God will allow you to have. We need to pray for an unveiling of His will so that we can begin to take in just how much God desires to use us, give us, and birth through us!

3. *Choose to associate with those who will take you into a commitment zone and out of your comfort zone.* That's what Elisha did for the Shunammite. That's what the friends of this blind man did for him.

Elisha didn't just speak destiny to the Shunammite—he was there to help her fulfill that destiny. When her son later became sick and died, Elisha was there to raise that boy back to life.

The blind man's friends didn't just *tell* the blind man about Jesus. They *led* him to Jesus.

Every person needs help becoming what God has called him to be. Nobody is born "polished." Every person needs to be developed. Ask God to bring people into your life who will polish and develop you in the way He desires.

God sent Jonathan into David's life. Jonathan knew how to be royalty. He knew how to be king. And God had prepared his heart so that Jonathan knew when to lay down his royal cloak at the feet of David and say, "I know the call of God is on *you* to be the king one day." God gave David a friend and mentor like Jonathan to prepare David for the destiny God had for him.

He'll do the same for you. Part of your preparation lies in the associations God leads you to make, nurture, and maintain. When God brings these people into your life to train you or polish you, don't send them away! Invite them into your life. Learn from them. Listen to them. It's up to you to develop those relationships.

4. *Choose to associate with those who will encourage you.* God desires that you "separate" yourself from people who come against you to distract you, detour you, and discourage you. Put some distance between yourself and those who speak discouragement into your life.

God's Word says, "A friend loves at all times" (Prov. 17:17). A true friend will not despise your weakness, but will believe for your strength. A true friend will not look down on you because of your past sin or failure, but will believe for your future glory in Christ Jesus. A true friend will encourage you.

There are people whom the devil sends to get us off track by discouraging us and despising us.

There comes a time when you have to stop listening to those who come to discourage or despise you . . . and just get on with the business of doing what it is that God tells you to do.

You may be looking at the deadness of your womb and other people may be telling you that you will never birth *anything*—that you will never produce life—and you may be discouraged. My word to you is this: Praise the Lord and go right ahead and give birth.

I saved for seven years to "birth" a television ministry. I had twenty-one thousand dollars of "she" money. "She" money is money that "he" knows about but doesn't get to spend. That's "she" money. I thought twenty-one thousand dollars was a lot of money. I didn't know how little it was when it came to television.

I was at a conference and the Holy Spirit began to move in an unusual way and the speaker began to call people to give. God spoke in my spirit, *Give twenty-five thousand dollars.*

I knew without a doubt that it was God speaking. Even so, I tried to negotiate with God. I tried to point out to Him that I had already been giving and that I didn't have twenty-five thousand dollars and that He had called me to start a television ministry . . . and do you know what happened? The more I tried to negotiate, the more I could see in my spirit that my dream of a television ministry was starting to wither and die inside my spiritual womb. What I saw with my spiritual eyes scared me. I finally turned to my husband and said, "God told me to give twenty-five thousand dollars. I need four thousand dollars of 'he' money.'"

I put his "he" money with my "she" money and laid it on the altar to obey the Lord. I wasn't expecting anything specific to come of that. I was just obeying what I knew God had told me to do. I knew my obedience was absolutely necessary to keep God's dream alive in my spiritual womb until it could be birthed. I didn't know how close I was to "delivery."

Within twenty-four hours I had a call from a man who operates a large Christian network of stations. He said, "I'm looking for this woman named Paula White." I said, "HERE SHE IS!"

It may seem that I appeared on Christian television overnight. That's only partly true. I spent twenty years of plowing the earth, preaching the gospel, and doing the gospel work . . . and then "overnight" I entered into my season of preaching on television. Pregnancy lasts nine months. Birthing can happen in a few hours.

God has a season for the birthing of the dream that you may have been carrying in your spiritual womb for years, perhaps even decades. Choose to develop associations with those who will encourage you to give birth and to cling to your dream until the birthing time arrives!

CHOOSE TRUTH

Choose today to start listening only to those who speak truth to you.

Start moving toward those who are walking in truth and have the anointing of God on their lives. Start moving toward those who have a lifestyle of faith and are prospering and whole in body, mind, and spirit. Begin to network with them. Start moving toward those who are moving toward the same destiny you believe God is calling you to pursue.

The truth is that you have treasure *inside you.* We each need people in our lives who can see the treasure inside us.

God's Word says, "Do you not know that your body is the temple of the Holy Spirit who is in you, whom you have from God?" (1 Cor. 6:19). The same God who stepped out on nothing and created everything is the God who lives inside you. Paul wrote, "We have this treasure in earthen vessels" (2 Cor. 4:7). We are not simply earthen vessels—cracked, chipped, and easily broken. We have treasure inside us that is eternal, glorious, and beyond value. We need people in our lives who believe that we are the temple of the Holy Spirit and that we have treasure inside us!

The truth is that you can achieve more than you've achieved, experience more than you have experienced, and have a greater anointing than you have.

We need people who have achieved more than we have achieved, who know God better than we know God, who have experienced life beyond what we have experienced. We need people who have greater faith than we have, a greater understanding of God's Word than we have, a greater anointing than what we have. We need to learn from them . . . and follow their examples.

The truth is that you have Christ in you, working through you. Every person has the same challenge and the same opportunity to release their full God-given potentials. It begins with the truth of Galatians 2:20, which says, "I have been crucified with Christ; it is no longer I who live, but Christ lives in me; and the life which I now live in the flesh I live by faith in the Son of God, who loved me and gave Himself for me." When Christ lives in you and you live by faith in Him, you are in a position to do "all things" by the strength He imparts to you (see Philippians 4:13). We must decrease so He may increase in our lives (see John 3:30).

We must choose the truth that Christ dwells in us, that He loves us and gave Himself for us, and that He lives in us and through us to touch others. When you develop the gift of God in you, you are a world changer and a history maker!

Do you sense in your heart today that you have been chosen as a daughter of destiny in the Lord, but you know in your spirit that you must break certain associations in your life for you to move *fully* into that destiny?

Deal with it!

Don't let wrong relationships delay your destiny any longer. Stop nurturing what needs to be neutered!

Determine today that there will be no more miscarriages of your destiny! No more detours! No more backing away from God's purpose for your life!

Determine today that you will not drag your past into your future and that you will cut off any associations that are not in keeping with God's plans and purposes for you.

Pray that God will send you the right spouse.

Pray that God will send the right people to speak into the lives of your children.

Pray that God will send intercessors into your life—people who will pray for you every day.

Pray that God will send those who can give into your life precisely what you need to prepare you to move into the next level God has for you.

Pray that God will send helpers alongside you.

Pray that God will send people who have the finances you need.

Trust God to strategically align your life with the right people so that you might move fully into the destiny He designed for you from the foundation of the world!

⌐ GOD'S WORD ON THE DAUGHTERS OF ZELOPHEHAD

These five sisters lived in the time of Moses and Joshua. Their father died, and the normal custom of the time was for sons to inherit the land of their fathers, and if there was no son, the land was to be divided among other male family members. Daughters were not given an inheritance. In this case, the land was "promised" land that had not yet been conquered. Zelophehad's daughters appealed the traditional property-rights custom to Moses, and then to Joshua . . . and won their case. The Scripture reference for this chapter is Numbers 27:1–7, and it is found in the Appendix to this book.

9

THE DAUGHTERS OF ZELOPHEHAD

"I have a hunch I'm being ripped off."

The five daughters of Zelophehad refused to lay back and let life rob them of their rightful inheritance. They refused to sit back and accept "wrongs" as part of their destiny. They were willing to challenge life!

Most people today are so passive and without passion that they do not seek out the power they need to press through the obstacles of life. The enemy wreaks havoc in their lives because they are passive to the point that they refuse to stand up and say, "Enough is enough!"

Passive people don't win in life. People expect that after they become Christians, everything will fall out of heaven into their laps. That isn't what God's Word says. Joshua 1:8 tells us that we become prosperous and successful when we speak God's Word, meditate on it day and night, and keep or observe it. It takes effort to speak, effort to read and study and meditate on God's Word, and effort to *do* the Word every day, day in and day out. Two-thirds of God's name is *Go*—you must put motion and effort and work to your faith.

There are some things in the Bible that we are to be spiritually violent about in the way we pray and confront the enemy of our souls. Jesus taught, "And from the days of John the Baptist until now the kingdom of heaven suffers violence, and the violent take it by force" (Matt. 11:12). I can be meek and mild about some things . . . but let me assure you this: you don't want to mess with me when it comes to my husband or my children or my health or the things that pertain to my destiny, or with my rightful inheritance before the Lord!

These five women challenged what had been handed to them and they *refused* to accept "wrong" as being "right." They believed their father had left them loaded, even if it was just being loaded with potential and promise.

Have you acknowledged and accepted the truth that your heavenly Father has left *you* loaded? Are you acting on the truth that your Father left you loaded?

YOUR FATHER LEFT YOU LOADED

Many of God's beloved children are dying from boredom and apathy. They haven't challenged what has been handed to them in life. They haven't challenged themselves to move into their God-given potentials and learn how to exercise and use their gifts. They aren't challenging the possibilities in their lives.

They haven't acted on the truths of God's Word. They haven't even begun to challenge and release the power God has put in them:

- "Which is Christ in you, the hope of glory" (1 Col. 1:27).

- "He who is in you is greater than he who is in the world" (1 John 4:4).

- "The Spirit of him who raised Jesus from the dead dwells in you" (Rom. 8:11).

The same God who stepped out of nothing into nothing and stood on nothing with nothing, and created *everything* is the God who dwells in you by the power of His Holy Spirit.

We worry about paying our electric bills and whether we will have a job tomorrow . . . but if we could ever tap into the potential and possibilities that God has placed inside us, anxieties such as those would have no part in us! God, in you, has power to bring things to you that you need.

Those who haven't challenged life and haven't challenged themselves live in frustration. Their frustration leads them to be angry with their spouses . . . angry with the economy . . . angry with the government. Their spouses, the economy, and the government are not the problem! The problem is that they haven't tapped into the well of life inside themselves.

The Tendency to Settle . . . The definition of *frustration* is "to settle for less than your destiny." When you are settling for less, something inside you begins to churn and to say, *This is not how I am supposed to live. This is not my destiny.* When your condition is contrary to your destiny, something inside you declares, *I'm greater than this. I can do more than this. I'm more valuable than this.*

Every person has a tendency to settle for "less"—it's human nature *not* to want to work hard at something or to challenge the status quo. It takes effort to get more education and to challenge the intellectual abilities we have been given. It takes effort to get more training to prepare for the better future God has for us. It takes courage to begin any project for which you don't have all the resources in place. It takes courage to step out of your comfort zone. God, however, always takes us out of our comfort zones. He always lays before us a challenge to do more, be more, and take on more. He lays before us a challenge that requires us to trust Him and then to act on our faith. He always calls us to stop settling for less.

. . . But a Desire for More. Even though we may have a tendency to settle for less, everybody still has a *desire* for more. If we didn't have that desire, we wouldn't find ourselves frustrated. We want other people to do more for us. We want man-made institutions and agencies and groups to do more for us. We want God to do more for us.

God says, "There is no more." When Jesus said, "It is finished" on the cross, He was declaring that He had given all there was to give. He had given us His life. He had made provision for us to receive the Holy Spirit. He had purchased for us all of the health and forgiveness and blessing we could ever receive and use. We don't need for God to give us anything more than what has already been given . . . we just need to learn how to walk in what has been accomplished on our behalf and released to us! God's Word assures us, "According as his divine power hath given unto us all things that pertain unto life and godliness, through the knowledge of him that hath called us to glory and virtue" (2 Peter 1:3 KJV).

When Jesus rose again from the dead and ascended into heaven and "sat down at the right hand of God," He was making a definitive statement that He had done everything He needed to do. He had done at Calvary "more than enough" for our deliverance, protection, provision, peace, and restoration. He didn't need to stand up again until the day when He would return to this earth (see Hebrews 10:12). God's Word says that from that moment when Jesus sat down at the right hand of the Father until *now*, He is "waiting till His enemies are made His footstool" (Heb. 10:13). Who will make His enemies His footstool? That's our part! That's our job! That's our role! We are the ones who are to receive all that Jesus purchased for us by His death and resurrection and take on the enemy of our souls and live out the fullness of the victory Jesus has given us!

DON'T DIE WITHOUT LIVING

What are you doing today to make your life matter . . . to make your life count for something . . . to make your life a life of importance and influence?

The book of James says, "For what is your life? It is even a vapor that appears for a little time and then vanishes away" (4:14). Go into any cemetery and on the gravestones you'll see the names of people who have died, and below their names, two dates—the dates of their births and the dates of their deaths—with a hyphen between the dates. The most important part of that person's life, however, does not lie in those dates. It lies in what happened in the hyphen! Ultimately, what's going to matter is the quality of life we live, the character we develop, and the legacy we leave.

What a shame to die without ever living! It would be an indictment for your epitaph to read, "A soul saved, but a life wasted."

God has a purpose for you every morning that you wake up on this earth. Every time you open your eyes and open your mouth, God has a purpose for what you see and what you say.

Great songs . . . great books . . . great sermons . . . great businesses . . . great acts of love and kindness . . . great deeds of heroism . . . and great witnesses for the gospel of Jesus Christ are in graveyards—they died without ever having been expressed or established. God's Word says, "A dream comes through much activity, and a fool's voice is known by his many words" (Eccl. 5:3). Dreams come to pass when we *work* our dreams and our potential, when we step out and challenge life and take on the possibilities that lie before us. If we are just sitting around thinking about or talking about our dreams and our potential, we will never move into our destiny—we will accomplish *nothing* and our dreams and our potential will go to the grave with us.

Your Father has already left you loaded! And if He left you loaded, why are you walking about in apathy or frustration? Why are you walking about with potential and promise buried in you, even if it isn't buried in your grave yet?

OVERCOMING THE FORCES OF DISCRIMINATION

The daughters of Zelophehad challenged a system that discriminated against them and left them feeling pressed down and frustrated. What they did was not popular or even accepted in their world. This was the first case of gender discrimination recorded in the Bible.

Many people today have been pressed down by discrimination—and I'm not referring only to racial discrimination. To *discriminate* means to "differentiate." It means to treat somebody with prejudice—which is a preconceived judgment or opinion—and to act in a different way toward that person. It means to judge a person as "different" and therefore, inferior.

Isn't it amazing that we human beings try so hard to fit in with other human beings, when it's our differences that make us valuable? Every person is a one-of-a-kind original. The moment after you were created, God broke the mold He used to create you. You are not a copy of any other person—past, present, or future. And, you are not to *imitate* any other person. A reporter once wrote that I'm a good-looking, feminine woman, but I preach like a man . . . I sound like I'm from Mississippi but I live in Florida . . . and I'm brave enough to preach about discrimination in the South. My *differences* are what make me unique and set me apart. I've learned to build on my differences.

It's one thing for you to accept your unique qualities and your "differences." It's another thing to have someone else discriminate against you because you are unique or "different."

Discrimination comes in lots of packages—ethnic discrimination, socioeconomic discrimination, gender discrimination, and discrimination related to various aspects of your life. Some people face discrimination because of things they've been through.

Years ago when Randy and I were just beginning our ministry and we were working in the projects and giving away virtually everything that came into our hands, there were days when I really *felt* poor. I was a little deceived at that time by the enemy. On most days in the projects, I was wearing jeans and a T-shirt, and I thought that if I could just have a new dress I'd *feel* better about myself and feel more feminine. I hadn't yet learned the truth of Ephesians 3:19, which says, "To know the love of Christ which passes knowledge; that you may be filled with all the fullness of God." I didn't know fulfillment comes with knowing you are loved by God. I thought fulfillment might have something to do with a new dress that didn't come from a thrift store.

So when the day came that I had a little money to buy a dress, I walked into a very nice dress store and I came face-to-face with discrimination. The clerks in that store wouldn't even look at me, much less talk to me! I picked out a couple of things to try on in the dressing room, and no clerk ever came to ask me if she might bring me a different dress or a different size. In fact, the clerks looked at me as if I were about to steal a dress rather than buy a dress. They saw my jeans and my T-shirt and automatically assumed I didn't have any money in my wallet and that I wasn't the type of woman who would either be interested in their clothes or be capable of affording their clothes.

I thought to myself, *You're looking at the outside of me and assuming that you know who I am. You don't have a clue who I am!* I knew that my current situation was just "seasonal"—my financial poverty was only temporary. I knew that according to God's Word, I was going to be blessed "in my coming in and going out" (see Deuteronomy 28:6). I didn't look anything like I was *going* to look.

Those clerks were only looking at my exterior *at that time.* They couldn't begin to see my potential and promise!

The reason discrimination hurts is because it includes rejection. *Rejection* means "to deny" or "to refuse to acknowledge" or "to cast aside or throw aside as being useless." A person who is rejected feels of less value. That person begins to feel less worthy.

But . . . if a person doesn't *need* the approval of other people, that person rarely "feels" rejection or the negative feelings associated with discrimination. The only way to not feel a need for other people's approval is if you know deep inside yourself that God approves of you and calls you valuable. You can survive discrimination if you know who you are in Christ.

You must recognize that people who deny you, refuse to acknowledge you, or reject you are people who don't have the ability to see the real you. On the basis of seeing just part of who you are, the world says, "You are less."

Only God has the ability to see all of you, from your beginning all the way to your ending, from your imperfection all the way to your perfection, and from where you are right now all the way to where you are going to be one day.

Only God knows you completely, and on the basis of the full information He has about you, He says, "You are more" (see Romans 8:37).

That's why God's opinion is the *only* opinion that really counts! That's why it's critically important that we know God's opinion and that we recognize we have already been fully accepted by God and are highly valued by God (see Ephesians 1:6).

When you know His opinion, you will associate with people who align themselves with God's thoughts for you.

Discrimination Is Rooted in Fear and Jealousy. People discriminate against other people because they are afraid that if another person is given the dignity and worth he deserves to have, they will "lose" something. If you get the promotion, they won't get it. If you get the job, they might lose their jobs. If you get a seat on the bus, they might not get a seat on the bus. If you get ahead, they might be left behind. Jealousy grows out of fear. As I have stated, it is the fear that someone or something can replace you.

Those who discriminate are afraid that if another person's dream comes true, their dream might not come true. If another person fulfills his potential and destiny, they might not be able to fulfill theirs. They have absolutely no understanding that God desires for *every* person to fulfill his potential and live out his destiny . . . have all the blessings that are given to those who are in covenant relationship with Him . . . and experience the presence of God every moment of every day of their lives. God is no respecter of persons—He does *not* discriminate, but freely and generously pours out His gifts to all people.

When you *know* that you are loved by God, you aren't nearly as concerned about who might not love you.

When you *know* that you are valued by God, you aren't nearly as concerned about who might not value you.

When you *know* that God calls you beloved and worthy, you aren't nearly as concerned about what other people might call you.

STAND UP AND STEP FORWARD

The daughters of Zelophehad didn't sit back because people loathed them . . . discriminated against them . . . rejected them from the inheritance of their father. They stepped up and stepped forward.

These five women are examples of encouragement to the weak and hope for the orphaned. They were cast aside, but they refused to be deprived of their inheritance.

Has somebody said to you, "Nobody will ever love you"? Have you sat down in that lie?

Has somebody said to you, "You aren't ministry material"? Have you sat down in that lie?

Has somebody said to you, "You'll never be more than a seven-dollar-an-hour employee"? Have you sat down in that lie?

Has somebody made you feel "less" because of your gender . . . because of your past . . . because of your condition . . . because of your race or ethnic background? Have you sat down in that lie?

Stand up and step forward! Step into the blessing and the destiny your heavenly Father has for you. He wants you to have *all* things that are rightfully yours—He wants you to have *all* things that the enemy has tried to keep from you and others have tried to deny you.

Zelophehad's name means "shadow of fear." In the Bible, names *mean* something—they stand for something. The "shadow of fear" is what Zelophehad grew up under. He was an Israelite wandering in the wilderness because his forefathers had been too afraid to go into the promised land. The shadow of fear in his own life had rested over his daughters.

The names of these five daughters of Zelophehad also have significant meaning:

Mahlah means "infirmity."

Noah means "wandering."

Hoglah means "turned from mourning to joyful dancing."

Milcah means "a queen."

Tirzah means "well-pleasing or acceptable."

What a tremendous progression of life we see in the names of these daughters! What a portrait of who we are and what we've been through.

Each of us began our lives in the shadow of fear. We began our lives as weak and infirm. From our births, we were separated from God. Any person who is separated from God is less than whole—he is weak in some way. He lives in emotional pain and spiritual sickness. God's Word tells us that we are born with a "fear of death" and that we are "subject to bondage" our entire lives because we live in fleshly bodies (Heb. 2:15). We are each born with a grief in our hearts over our sin-stricken states.

In our infirmity, we wander through life. We have no direction, no strong pursuit of our promise or destiny. We look for help and comfort . . . very often, in all the wrong places and from all the wrong people.

But Jesus passes by and finds us! He speaks life to us and turns our mourning to joy and dancing. He doesn't pull us from the field, but in that field where He finds us and causes us to thrive, He establishes us as His queen. God's Word says you are the apple of God's eye (Ps. 17:8). He has made you royalty—He "has made us kings and priests" (Rev. 1:6). Jesus is King of kings and He has chosen you to be part of His bride—the bride of a King is a *queen*.

He has loved you and continues to love you, and in His great love for you, He calls you well-pleasing and acceptable in His sight.

The names of these daughters represent our covenant with God. Their names portray the full inheritance we have from God.

Instead of infirmity . . . our heavenly Father gives us wholeness.

Instead of wandering . . . our heavenly Father gives us direction and destiny. He gives us purpose and fulfillment.

Instead of mourning and sadness over what has been . . . our heavenly Father gives us joy about what can be and what will be.

Instead of a self-perception of being worthless . . . our heavenly Father tells us we are royalty.

Instead of a devaluing, hopeless, and helpless feeling that we are nothing and never will be anything . . . our heavenly Father gives us love and counts us so valuable that He sent His only Son to die on a cross so we could live with Him forever.

Your heavenly Father does not call you by the shame of your past or your current condition. He calls you by your name and your position *in Christ*.

Anticipate Opposition. These five daughters of Zelophehad went together to challenge the system. What they did was unacceptable and unpopular in their time.

When you move into your destiny—walking out your covenant with God and living in your rightful position in Christ—you are going to face opposition. The devil will hate you even more than he does now. People who are manipulated by the devil will move against you.

If you get out of the boat and begin to walk on water, everybody who is still in the boat will try to call you back into the boat or ridicule you for what you are stepping out to do. If people cannot control you, manipulate you, or duplicate you, they will try to kill you. They will do everything in their power to *stop* you from moving forward into your destiny. But . . . Jesus is calling you to step out of the boat and walk on water. He has already accepted you. He has given you life. He has caused you to thrive. He has entered into a covenant relationship with you. He is taking you from infirmity and wandering and mourning to dancing for joy as a queen who is well-pleasing and acceptable in His eyes!

THE POWER OF A REQUEST

The daughters of Zelophehad operated in the power of a request. God's Word says, "You do not have because you do not ask" (James 4:2). Jesus taught, "Whatever things you ask in prayer, believing, you will receive" (Matt. 21:22).

There's tremendous power in a request. A person who knows what to ask and when to ask and how to ask is difficult to turn down! The Bible says about a virtuous woman, "She opens her mouth with wisdom, and on her tongue is the law of kindness" (Prov. 31:26).

There is a way to challenge any system by making a request, and there is a way to make a request without violating any principles.

We are not to make requests in anger or bitterness, with a spirit of unforgiveness, or with doubt or anxiety (see Philippians 4:6 and James 1:6–8).

We are to make our requests with boldness, love, wisdom, and kindness (see Hebrews 4:16).

God has given women a gift of communication. Women are more verbal, while men are more physical. A woman says what she feels and expresses her love in words. A man is more likely to express what he feels with a pat on the back or a firm handshake.

We need to recognize the gift of communication we have been given by God, thank God for this gift, and then learn how to use this gift and become skillful in it. We must learn how to approach a person, how to make a request in an effective way, and how to time our requests for the maximum amount of impact.

We also need to recognize that God has given women the gift of *influence*. What we women say to our husbands and children carries weight—what we say influences them even if they act at times as if they aren't hearing us. Influence is speaking and acting in a way that causes a person to act in a particular way— it is the ability to affect a person or an event. Influence is neutral. It can be used for either good or bad. For influence to be effective for good *over time*, a woman needs to become skillful in making her requests so that she doesn't "win an argument" but "lose the war." Just as important as using words to make requests is knowing when to be silent.

God's Word is filled with examples of the influence of women, for both good and evil:

- Eve spoke to Adam . . . she influenced him to eat fruit from the tree of the knowledge of good and evil.

- Sarai spoke to Abram . . . she influenced him to sleep with her maid, Hagar.

- Abigail spoke to David . . . she influenced him to with-
hold the sword from the house of Nabal, thus saving her
life and also preserving David's future reputation and
authority as king.

For you fully to live out what God has destined for you, you must
become willing to speak up when God asks you to speak up. You must
be willing to step out when God asks you to step out. You must be
willing to challenge the system with your skillful requests. You must
be willing to express yourself in a bold, wise, loving, and kind manner
in spite of public opinion . . . in spite of discriminating attitudes . . .
and in spite of the way you may have been rejected in the past.

Know Your Inheritance. Your request must be *your* request. You must
request what you know to be *your* inheritance.

The daughters of Zelophehad knew their inheritance. They
didn't go before Moses and ask for something that wasn't rightfully
theirs. They went requesting what they believed God had promised
to them was *their inheritance.* Moses went before the Lord with their
request and came back saying, "You're right. You shall have the possession of inheritance among your father's brothers." He *confirmed*
the promise of God to their hearts.

Not only that, but the law regarding inheritance was changed
because of what these daughters of Zelophehad requested and God
confirmed to Moses. God's Word tells us that the Lord said to Moses,
"You shall speak to the children of Israel, saying: 'If a man dies and
has no son, then you shall cause his inheritance to pass to his daughter.'" This word of the Lord became a statute of judgment for all the
children of Israel (see Numbers 27:8).

You need to know what it is that God has promised to *you.*
Among those promises are the things that God promises to *all* those
who have accepted Jesus as their Savior and are following Him as

their Lord. Among those promises are the things God promises to all who are keeping His commandments and meditating on His Word and speaking His Word. Among those promises are the things God has spoken to your own heart . . . things that are specifically for *you*.

One of the ways you can know those things are specifically for you is through the confirmation of what the Bible speaks to you on that matter, and also what God speaks to your heart as you pray about the matter.

Go to God's Word and ask the Lord as you read and study it, "What are my rights? What is it You have for *me?* What is *my* inheritance?"

Refuse to Develop a Victim Mentality. As you study God's Word to determine your rightful inheritance and God's promise to *you*, refuse and deny the tendency to develop a victim mentality. The enemy will come to you again and again to whisper into your life, "You don't deserve that. You can't have that. Other people will keep you from that."

A victim mentality says, "I can't get out unless you let me out. I can't succeed unless you let me succeed."

God says, "I've already purchased for you your freedom and your success. All things are possible to you because You have *Me*, and all things are possible in Me."

When you find yourself in a discriminating, frustrating situation, don't start criticizing everybody around you. Don't start blaming others for what you believe they are doing to you. Don't adopt the victim mentality that gives power to other people to control your destiny or keep you from succeeding. Stand up on the inside and declare, "I'm going to pursue what God has for me *regardless* of what others say or do."

If God promises you peace, don't settle for anxiety and worry and stress.

If God promises you renewed strength and joy, don't settle for debilitating exhaustion and frustration.

If God promises you godly relationships, don't settle for ungodly ones.

Go to God's Word and ask the Lord, "What do You have for me?"

When you get His answer to your heart, act on that answer. Claim that inheritance!

PURSUE THE PASSION OF YOUR TRUE SELF

The dream and passion in your heart is a major part of God's inheritance for you. The pursuit of your dream and passion is what will give you fulfillment.

I have always taught my children to find their passion and then figure out a way to make money as they pursue it. In your passion, you will find your purpose and have the power to fulfill it. Where people make a mistake is that they get jobs and then try to find a way to work at their passions around the edges and on weekends and late at night. They are frustrated because they aren't focused on what they truly dream of doing, love to do, and know God has prepared and gifted them to do.

If you dread getting up and going to work on Monday morning, ask yourself, "Why am I working at this job?" Find a job that you can hardly wait to get to! There are plenty of jobs in this world, plenty of ways to make money. Pursue your *God-given* passion as your first priority.

You may need to downsize some of the trappings of your life as you make the transition to the pursuit of your passion and dream. Consider that transition a temporary season for your life. My husband, Randy, used to hold me in the middle of the night as we began our ministry in Tampa and had nothing. He'd say, "Sacrifice with me now, Paula, and I'll give you a great future." I had no problem accepting those words and believing them. I had a mind-set that Randy and I were doing what God had told us to do. I knew our material and financial situation at that time was temporary. There are periods and seasons when we must sacrifice in order to plant the seeds we need to plant . . . to produce the harvest that we desire to see.

Take a new look at how you are spending your time and resources. Are you building something? Are you willing to sacrifice today for the tomorrow you know God has planned for you? Are you willing to give now so you can receive later?

Your Dreams, Your Inheritance. Don't live your life to fulfill the expectations or desires of another person. Live your life in pursuit of the dream God has put in *your* life—a dream only *you* can pursue and only *you* can fulfill.

I know millionaires, even billionaires, who are miserable because they haven't been true to themselves. They haven't been their "true selves" and therefore, they aren't living authentic lives. They are pursuing goals other people have set for them and passions other people have expressed to them. We are not called to fulfill other people's dreams. We are called to fulfill the dreams God has planted in us.

"But isn't that a selfish life?" you may be saying.

No.

There's no difference between your "true" self and God's plan for you. Your true self is made up of your deepest desires and gifts and abilities and dreams and passions. Your true self is what God created in you. It is *who* God made you to be.

Selfishness is not a matter of pursuing your true self. Selfishness is when you stop giving to others and when you keep *all* of the harvest you reap for your own pleasures.

Instead of accepting the limits that have been placed on you—including the limits you have placed on yourself—challenge the system and pursue your passion!

Instead of accepting the way it's always been done—even if that way puts people down and perpetuates prejudice—challenge the system and pursue your passion!

Instead of settling for less than you know is rightfully yours before God—challenge the system and pursue your passion!

For years my mother worked in health care. She pursued all the education she needed and developed her skills and became superb at hospital administration. She went to the top in her field.

When her retirement years came, my mother switched gears. She had always loved antiques, and she became what we teasingly called "a junk lady." She began to buy items at estate sales and resell them in a shop of her own. She loved it. Then she decided that she didn't need a shop to buy and sell antiques—she could do that over the Internet. And she does, very successfully. I have never seen my mother happier in her work or more fulfilled in what she does from dawn to dusk. She is always in pursuit of a "find" and always excited at a profitable sale. She sets her own schedule and makes enough to have a good living. Most of all, she is at peace. She knows Jesus as her Savior, she knows His peace in her life, and she knows she is being true to her God-given gifts.

I said to her one day, "You put yourself through over ten years of school to become a junk lady? You worked for decades to get to the top of a field that you didn't really love?"

She just smiled. My mother is doing today what she loves to do. She has found her passion and is pursuing it. That's success.

Are you expressing your true self today?

Are you pursuing *your* God-given passion and destiny?

Are you experiencing the fulfillment and success that is part of your inheritance? Or . . .

Are you feeling put down . . . pressed down . . . or kept down? If so . . .

Deal with it!

Your heavenly Father has left you loaded with potential and promise. He has given you a tremendous inheritance in Christ Jesus. Your inheritance cost the Father the price of His only begotten and beloved Son's life!

Accept your inheritance. Refuse to live beneath your covenant privileges. Begin to make your requests known to the Father. Make your requests known to those to whom He directs you. Become skillful and wise in making your requests.

Become a woman who leaves a legacy of influence on this world!

Rip off the labels. Rip off the limitations and mediocrity. Challenge life and trust God as you pursue His best.

⌒ GOD'S WORD ON ESTHER

Esther was a displaced, orphaned, Jewish girl—raised in Persia by an older relative named Mordecai. She was chosen by King Ahasuerus to be queen. When Haman, one of the king's advisors, plotted in his hatred to kill all Jews in Persia, Esther faced her possible destruction and the potential loss of her position in the palace. The Scripture reference for this chapter is Esther 4:13–14, and it is found in the Appendix to this book.

10

ESTHER

"Why is this happening to me?"

Esther was an extraordinary woman. To be extraordinary means to be great . . . out of the box . . . a woman who is great for God and who has a purpose and destiny for her life.

This extraordinary woman was in a crisis. Just because someone is extraordinary doesn't mean that she can't experience a crisis.

Have you ever been in a crisis?

Have you discovered that the child you raised up to be a godly person is now smoking weed?

Have you discovered that the husband you have been faithful to for decades has come home smelling like another woman's cologne with a love note in his pocket that is not in your handwriting?

Have you just heard that the job you have done well for years is now being "phased out" or transferred to a distant city?

Have you just heard that your team has not picked you up for another season . . . or that your child has *not* been going to school every day as you thought . . . or that the routine test at the doctor's office didn't turn out the way you were sure it would?

Countless millions of people are in crisis on any given day. A crisis is a turning point for better or worse. A crisis is a decisive moment when any situation has reached the point of being critical. Crises occur when the future is at stake. That's the situation in which Esther found herself.

The question posed to Esther was a powerful one: "Who knows whether you have come to the kingdom for such a time as this?"

Could it be that your crisis is a catalyst for a greater role or position?

Could it be that your "pit" is preparing you for the "palace"?

Could it be God is positioning *you* for a greater purpose?

Who knows . . . like Esther you may have come to God's kingdom for such a time as this!

GOD HAS SUSTAINED YOU

Have you been abused and misused, forsaken and forgotten, broken and battered? If so, the truth of your life is that God has sustained you and brought you to this point.

You haven't arrived where you are today by your great ability, education, family background, social position, intellect, beauty, skills, or sheer willpower. You are where you are today because God has kept you and sustained you.

Our amazing God with His amazing grace has sustained you for His purposes. He has saved you, given you a testimony, called you, and raised you up for this very moment, this very opportunity, this very challenge!

He is your strength! God's Word says, "My God shall be My strength" (Isa. 49:5).

He is your refuge! God's Word says the Lord is "my strength and my fortress, my refuge in the day of affliction" (Jer. 16:19).

He is your rock and defender! The Bible says, "He only is my rock and my salvation; He is my defense; I shall not be greatly moved" (Ps. 62:2).

Don't deceive yourself. You are who you are and where you are because of Him.

When you know with certainty that God has sustained you to

this point and that God has *more* for you in your future than anything in your yesterday, then you have the strength to persevere through any crisis that comes your way. You hold on. You refuse to give up. You live in the anticipation that your greater blessing is on its way!

Anytime you think you might not make it, you need to remind yourself of God's Word:

- "Nay, in all these things we are more than conquerors through him that loved us" (Rom. 8:37).

- "Now thanks be unto God, which always causes us to triumph in Christ, and maketh manifest the savor of his knowledge by us in every place" (2 Cor. 2:14).

- "For whatsoever is born of God overcometh the world: and this is the victory that overcometh the world, even our faith" (1 John 5:4).

Our strength comes from God—it's not something we work up in ourselves. We can do all things *through Christ*. It is God's strength poured into us and working through us that enables us to overcome, to persevere, and to be strong. We come to strength by resting in Him.

Whatever it is that you perceive and desire . . . you can accomplish and do *through Christ*.

You *can* be the mother you desire to be.

You *can* do the job of your dreams.

You *can* win nations for Christ.

You *can* break the bondage and poverty of welfare.

You *can* have a functional family and a loving marriage.

I don't know what you may be going through right now, but I know this, *Christ in you* makes you strong enough to handle it!

QUALITIES THAT MAKE A PERSON
EXTRAORDINARY

There are qualities that made Esther extraordinary—qualities that are worthy of close examination because they are the precepts and principles that God uses in preparing each one of us for His purpose.

What are these qualities? Let me share seven of them with you:

1. *No Bitterness over Brokenness.* Esther experienced some brokenness in her life, but she was not bitter.

Everybody experiences some brokenness in life. One of the earliest nursery rhymes many of us learned was that Humpty Dumpty sat on a wall and Humpty Dumpty had a great fall. All the king's horses and all the king's men couldn't put Humpty Dumpty back together again. All the king's horses and all the king's men can't put *you* back together again, either.

No person can put you back together after you are broken by life. Only God can go into the depths of your soul and put together the broken fragments of your life in a way that restores your capacity to love and to trust and to believe.

Esther came from what we would call a dysfunctional family. She was an orphan, a Jewish girl who was called Hadassah, which means "myrtle." She was later renamed Esther, which means "star."

Any time you change the name of a child, you impact the identity of that child. You raise questions in the child's mind, "Who am I?" There are countless adults today who are wondering who they are because they are wondering who their fathers were. There are thousands upon thousands of children who are living in foster homes and adopted homes who don't know who their parents are, who their grandparents are, or who their siblings are. Esther didn't allow all the changes in her life to strip away her God-given identity.

The story of Esther is a lesson to all of us that a person with a past can touch God in the present and believe Him to give her a future. Not every person will do that. Some people who love God remain bitter and broken. But every person *has the opportunity* to touch God and believe for restoration in their areas of depletion.

Esther's mother and father had died. They had been among the captives led away from Jerusalem by Nebuchadnezzar. She knew difficult times—an environment of slavery and oppression in her early childhood. She was brought up by her cousin, Mordecai.

Life was not "fair" to Esther. But . . . Esther refused to become bitter even though she had been broken and depleted by life.

The truth is that life does deplete us. It takes our energy . . . saps our strength . . . drains our creativity . . . dries out our enthusiasm and hope . . . draws upon our emotions . . . and siphons off our resources. It *depletes* us. And depleted people often do crazy things to try to fill up what has been drained from them. Their "love" tank gets a little low and they sleep with the next person that comes along. Their "peace" or "friendship" tanks get a little low, and in search of comfort or acceptance, they turn to alcohol for comfort. Depleted people become hurting and desperate people. But . . . God offers us restoration. God's Word says, "He restores my soul" (Ps. 23:3).

God has a "now" word to heal your past situations and hurts. He has restoration for those areas of your life that have been fragmented, ripped, and raped in your life. No amount of a false religion or a self-help course can do in a lifetime what God can do with just one touch of His hand on your life. You cannot restore yourself. No other person can restore you but Jesus.

God's Word says:

So I will restore to you the years that the swarming locust
    has eaten,
The crawling locust,
The consuming locust,

And the chewing locust,

My great army which I sent among you.

You shall eat in plenty and be satisfied,

And praise the name of the LORD your God,

Who has dealt wondrously with you;

And My people shall never be put to shame.

Then you shall know that I am in the midst of Israel:

I am the LORD your God

And there is no other.

My people shall never be put to shame. (Joel 2:25–27)

You must allow God's love to pierce your pain and heal you and make you whole. You must refuse to allow the enemy to rob you of *good* moments in your present because of *bad* moments in your past.

If you allow the enemy to keep you living in past bad moments, you will never be whole, and you *need* to be whole in order to fully embrace and live out the future God has for you. Refuse to be bitter over brokenness! Let God's love *restore you!*

When He restores you, God gives you purpose in place of years of question marks. That's what Genesis 50:20 is all about. Among Joseph's last words to the brothers who had sold him into slavery were these: "You meant evil against me; but God meant it for good, in order to bring it about as it is this day, to save many people alive." Many times, man's plans for us are rooted in evil, but God is working all the time to bring about your restoration so that when we look back, we can see His hand at work. We can see that He was with us all the time, delivering us and then restoring us so that we could see many people saved and alive for eternity! You may not understand the purpose of the pain as you go through it, but one day you will understand it. There is a purpose far greater than anything you can imagine.

And how do you know that the pit in which you were put

was not the stepping stone to the palace? How do you know that the palace wasn't even about *you*, but about God's plan to use you to experience the palace and bring about deliverance for others? Mordecai asked Esther, "Who knows whether you have come to the kingdom *for such a time as this?*"

When God restores you, He brings you to wholeness. He gives you the courage to love again . . . the courage to face life . . . the ability to experience life fully. Out of your wholeness, you are able to love the unlovable, to be brave in the face of terror, and to trust even after years of not being able to trust.

Don't miss out on your opportunity to experience God's best in your life because you are focused on the worst of your life.

Begin to appreciate God's restoring power. Open yourself up to His restoring love.

2. *Submission to Authority.* Esther had a second rare quality—she was independent yet submissive. Submission isn't a quality we like to talk about in women's circles today, but there's safety, freedom, and protection in submission. I am grateful that my husband is the head of our home and that he has the responsibility and authority over our household. He goes out and wins the paycheck, which means he is a "conqueror" and men are created to be conquerors. But he brings that paycheck home and hands it over to Mama to spend wisely for our provision, and that gives me a feeling of safety, freedom, and protection. He is the final decision maker. He listens to my counsel, considers my feelings, and with the wisdom of God, chooses what he feels is best for the family. Submission is easy if you are under the authority of a person who loves you as Christ loves the church!

Esther was elevated to the position of queen. She was a chosen woman with her own quarters in the palace and her own servants. But she still remained teachable and submissive to others who were in authority. When Esther first went to the king's palace she was put "under the custody of Hegai" (Est. 2:8). She submitted to everything Hegai told her to do—he was in charge of her preparation for an audience with the king. That preparation time included six months with oil of myrrh, and six months with perfumes and preparations for beautifying women. For twelve months, Esther took this man's instructions. He taught her *exactly* what the king would like. She only did what he advised (Est. 2:15). And to a great degree, because Esther submitted herself to Hegai's instruction, she knew how to please the king as no other woman knew how to please him. In the end, this woman who wisely submitted to authority was chosen to be the queen.

Esther also took instruction from Mordecai, her cousin, who "sat within the king's gate." Every day, Mordecai "paced in front of the court of the women's quarters, to learn of Esther's welfare and what was happening to her." Mordecai had instructed Esther to not reveal her people or her family. She listened to what he said (see Esther 2:10–11, 21).

Order is the accurate, effective, and productive arrangement of things. When a person is out of order—when a person seeks to get out from under the authority that has been placed over them—chaos results. Esther placed herself under Mordecai's authority as the man who had raised her and instructed her in the Word of God. She placed herself under Hegai's authority as the man who could help her in practical matters to win the king's favor. She had an understanding of protocol and she followed it.

God desires order for His church . . . for the family . . . for an individual's life. There is a chain of authority that He has put in place so we can be effective and productive and without chaos in our lives. God operates through authority. It's pride that causes a person to get out of order. Esther didn't give in to pride—even after she was named queen. She remained submissive and I honor her for that.

3. *Inner Confidence to Handle Pressure.* A third quality that made Esther extraordinary is that she had a great inner confidence that gave her the ability to handle pressure.

We live in a pressure-filled world. Pressure doesn't care if you are rich or poor, black or white, male or female. Pressure hits all of us—some of us are hit with pressure all of the time, and all of us are hit with pressure some of the time.

Esther was in a pressurized situation. She had known pressure as a little girl when she was taken from her homeland. She had known pressure when her parents died. She knew pressure now when she was taken into the king's palace, where she was up against women from 127 provinces, all of them vying to be queen. The king had said, "Let the king give her royal position to another who is better than she" (Est. 1:19). "She" in that verse is Vashti, the former queen. Queen Vashti was "beautiful to behold" (1:11). Esther wasn't only up against the stiff competition of 127 beautiful virgin girls, but she was also up against the remembrance of the beautiful former queen!

Pressure is not necessarily a bad thing. Pressure can make us produce. The challenge of pressure is learning how to handle it, and Esther learned that lesson.

But look how confident Esther was! When Esther went into the presence of the king, she "requested nothing." The other girls went into the king's presence needing many ornaments and other items that they thought would appeal to the king. They beautified their exterior. Esther went with what was inside her—she went to this man with inner strength that radiated beauty (Est. 2:15).

I know that men are "sight-stimulated"—they respond to a beautiful exterior—but there is something absolutely stunning and radiantly beautiful about a woman who has inner strength. God's Word says, "Do not let your adornment be merely outward—arranging the hair, wearing gold, or putting on fine apparel—rather let it be the hidden person of the heart, with the incorruptible beauty of a gentle and quiet spirit, which is very precious in the sight of God" (1 Peter 3:3–4).

Beauty fades. It *always* fades. A man might be drawn to that woman who pumps up her breasts and puts on her high heels and struts her stuff. But forty years down the line, she's going to look like her mama. After she has had three babies and done the work of raising them and gravity has taken its toll, those breasts are going to sag and no matter how much toner she uses, she's going to have wrinkles and stretch marks, and she may be strutting her stuff, but not in four-inch heels.

Invest in what God has put *inside* you. Don't invest in what fades. Invest in what lasts all through life and on into eternity! God doesn't want emotional nuclear waste inside you to spew out of you and contaminate others around you. He doesn't want hatred, anger, bitterness, or criticism flowing out of you. He doesn't want a controlling, manipulative spirit flowing from you. God wants the inside of you to be a "river of living water" flowing out to minister life and refreshment to others (see John 7:38).

Devote your time and energy to developing yourself from the inside out. Come to the awareness of who is in you and what He says you are and will be and will do.

Esther was not intimidated. She could handle a hostile environment because she knew who God had made her to be. She was strong on the inside.

4. *A Willingness to Undergo the Process of Preparation.* God's Word tells us that each young woman went in to King Ahasuerus after she had completed twelve months' *preparation* (Est. 2:12).

Preparation is the process that begins with a promise and ends with full provision. Preparation is a series of actions that lead to a determined end.

Who are you looking to for your preparation?

Are you calling the psychic hotline?

Are you reading the horoscope in the morning newspaper?

Are you going to the mall to buy a five-thousand-dollar wardrobe that you hope will "prepare" you to be confident on any occasion?

Are you calling a friend every other minute asking, "What should I do? What should I say? How should I handle this?"

Prepare yourself by going to God! Go to God's Word and immerse yourself in it. You must make a decision that you will choose God's direction for your life. Discipline yourself and make a determination in your heart that you will persevere in the preparation until you move into your destiny. Get into the Word and stay in the Word.

Prepare yourself with those things that will prepare you to enter the presence of a holy God.

The process of preparation is just that—a *process*. The journey in this life is just as important as the destination. God does not refine you, train you, transform you, or renew you instantly. He puts you through a *process*. That process requires patience. It requires a steadfastness and a faithfulness. It requires an ongoing trust and obedience.

You can't prepare yourself in a day. You must prepare yourself *every* day . . . day after day after day after day . . . for the rest of your days.

5. *Seeking God's Wisdom.* Wisdom is knowing what to say, and when to say it. In Esther's life, the day came when Mordecai overheard that two of the king's eunuchs and doorkeepers, Bigthan and Teresh, were furious and were plotting to lay hands on King Ahasuerus. He told Queen Esther about this and "Esther informed the king in Mordecai's name" (Est. 2:22). Esther knew when to speak up and when to be silent.

There were no doubt many things that Esther "heard" in the

palace—both fact and rumor—but this particular piece of information she passed on. Not everything you hear needs to be passed on to someone in higher authority . . . but some things do need to be passed on—especially when it interferes with destiny or the fulfillment of a vision. It takes wisdom to know when to speak up and when to keep quiet.

Knowledge comes from study, but wisdom comes from God. Every one of us needs more of God's wisdom. God's Word tells us, "If any of you lacks wisdom, let him ask of God, who gives to all liberally and without reproach, and it will be given to him" (James 1:5). We must do the asking. Only God can give us the insight and understanding about how to walk in *His* ways and accomplish *His* destiny for our life. Wisdom is the comprehensive insight into the ways and purposes of God.

Life is not a series of earning paychecks, having children, buying cars and houses, and then dying. Life is not a house on the beach and a boat in the dock. Life is not a career. God has a bigger and better purpose than that—He sets the goals of eternity before you. Wisdom is necessary if you are going to get your eyes off the here and now and focus them on God's bigger picture for the "now and forever."

Good plans are not always God's plans.

Get God's wisdom for *your* life!

6. *Getting the Necessary Information.* Esther was aware of her surroundings. Esther's maids and eunuchs came and told her that Mordecai had torn his clothes and had put on sackcloth and ashes, and that he was going through the city crying out with a loud and bitter voice, even to the point that he came to the king's gate (see Esther 4:1–4).

How can we take a city unless we know what ails a city? We are called to tear down strongholds in prayer, but how do we know what to pray for unless we become informed?

How can we meet the needs of a city unless we become informed about what those needs might be?

God called the prophet Ezekiel to be in the presence of the captives at Tel Abib, and Ezekiel said, "I sat where they sat, and remained there astonished among them seven days." After that, the word of the Lord came to Ezekiel telling him what he was to say (see Ezekiel 3:15–17). You need to know the people to whom God is sending you with His Word.

I speak internationally. To be effective, I need to be informed about the needs of the people to whom God sends me. I need to know what is going on in their nation, what problems they are facing, and what they are being taught or told by their leaders.

It's very easy to criticize something if you don't *understand* what's going on in that person's life, or in that culture, or in that nation.

How big is your sphere of influence? If you are called to minister to your neighborhood, know your neighborhood. If you are called to win your city, know your city. If you are called to win America, know America. If you are called to win the world, know the world! Read as much as you can and as often as you can. Educate yourself! Get in a conversation that intimidates you. Cause your mind to be stretched. Cross-pollinate. Meet people who are not just like you. Information gives you the power to make quality decisions.

7. *Troubled by the Troubles of Others . . . to the Point of Action.* When Esther heard what Mordecai was doing, she was "deeply distressed" (Est. 4:4).

There are people all around you who are suffering. God's people aren't immune from suffering. God's Word tells us, " May the God of all grace, who called us to His eternal glory by Christ Jesus, after you have suffered a while, perfect, establish, strengthen, and settle you" (1 Peter 5:10). Now, I don't believe that God *sends* suffering to perfect, establish, strengthen, and settle us. But I do believe that *when* we suffer, God can *use* our suffering to perfect, establish, strengthen, and settle us.

Watch how people respond to those who are going through trouble. Do they respond with mercy and compassion? Choose to associate yourself with people who are troubled by the troubles of others and who move to help them. The day will come when you *need* a friend who will show mercy and compassion to you. For your part, *be* that person of mercy and compassion to others.

Esther *could* have ignored Mordecai. But she didn't. Esther sent garments to clothe Mordecai and take his sackcloth away from him.

We are commanded to take action. God's Word says, "Be doers of the word, and not hearers only" (James 1:22). If we are hearers only, we deceive ourselves.

God's Word also says, "What does it profit, my brethren, if someone says he has faith but does not have works? Can faith save him? If a brother or sister is naked and destitute of daily food, and one of you says to them, 'Depart in peace, be warmed and filled,' but you do not give them the things which are needed for the body, what does it profit? Thus also faith by itself, if it does not have works, is dead" (James 2:14–17).

When you see a need, reach out to meet it. In meeting that need, you will be in a position to receive what God has to meet *your* needs. As you walk in obedience to God in caring for others, God will unlock doors to your provision. God does for you what you do for others.

DON'T MISS YOUR MOMENT

Mordecai asked Esther, "Who knows whether you have come to the kingdom for such a time as this?"

Why develop the seven qualities I have listed above? Why choose to become an *extraordinary* woman?

Because God has something extraordinary for you to do!

Don't miss the moment for which God has prepared you.

Everything that you have gone through in your life has brought you to *this* moment so you might be a person who can influence and change your world for God.

You have been chosen to change the atmosphere of your world.

Where there is torment . . . you are to bring God's peace.

Where there is confusion . . . you are to bring God's wisdom and truth in clarity.

Where there is hell . . . you are to bring the message and hope of heaven.

Are you wondering about your purpose? Are you wondering why certain things have happened to you in the past, or are happening to you today?

God is preparing you! He is transforming you into a person who will rise above bitterness and be overflowing with God's love. He is transforming you into a person who is independent and strong, yet submissive to His authority at all times. He is establishing in you the ability to withstand pressure and to have an inner confidence that comes from a relationship with Him.

Mordecai said to Esther, "Relief and deliverance will arise" . . . but in his great statement of faith was the implied question . . . "but will that relief and deliverance come through you, Esther?" (see Esther 4:14).

God's desire today is to bring relief and deliverance to His people. But will that relief and deliverance come through *you?*

Will you have anything to do with the healing that God desires to bring to a person who is sick physically, emotionally, mentally, or spiritually?

Will you have a part in meeting the needs that God desires to meet?

Will you win the souls that God desires to be won?

Will you be the one who speaks what God desires to be spoken?

Will you be the one who does what God desires to be done?

If you don't have a strong sense of your purpose and destiny today . . .

Deal with it!

Ask God to reveal to you what it is that He has as your destiny in life. Ask Him to give you a glimpse of the future He has already prepared for you. It's a future bathed in the glory of God . . . and it's a destiny worth pursuing with your whole heart.

CONCLUSION

THE WORD AND THE WORK

Mirror, mirror, on the wall . . .

These women of the Bible challenge us to "see" what is inside us—not only to look at the surface of our lives, but to see deep within. They challenge us to confront life's issues and deal with them. The process may be painful at times, but it is always therapeutic. It always has the potential for healing us and making us whole.

The Bible tells us that the Word of God is "living and powerful, and sharper than any two-edged sword, piercing even to the division of soul and spirit, and of joints and marrow, and is a discerner of the thoughts and intents of the heart" (Heb. 4:12). God's Word reveals to us our sins, our shortcomings, our failures, and faults—not with the intent that we live in guilt and condemnation, but that we repent of our sins, overcome our shortcomings, and deal with our failures and faults. God's desire for us is that we grow into the perfection of the full stature of Christ Jesus in our character, our habits, our attitudes, and our responses to life's circumstances. God's Word holds out to us the great hope that we can be changed into the image of the "glory of the Lord" and that the process is just that—a process of growth "from glory to glory" by the Spirit of the Lord (2 Cor. 3:18).

If you are willing to identify, confront, and conquer the issues of your life—to truly *deal with them*—God will heal you, restore you, and lead you into the destiny that He has planned for you, a destiny that is beyond your wildest dream.

A key principle, however, that we must never overlook or undervalue, is that *we* must be willing to deal with our issues. God will reveal to us what He desires to see changed in us. He will reveal to us the destiny He has planned and prepared for us. He will help us as we make the effort to deal with our issues. But God will not do the work of confronting and changing. We are the ones who must become "doers of the word, and not hearers only" (James 1:22). If we only see our image in the mirror and do nothing about what we see, we deceive ourselves—we continue to live in the lies of the devil, continue to fall into old patterns of behavior and thinking, and continue to experience failure and defeat. The challenge and promise of God's Word is this:

> If anyone is a hearer of the word and not a doer, he is like a man observing his natural face in a mirror; for he observes himself, goes away, and immediately forgets what kind of man he was.
>
> But he who looks into the perfect law of liberty and continues in it, and is not a forgetful hearer but a doer of the work, this one will be blessed in what he does. (James 1:23–25)

God calls us to hear and study His *Word* so that we might do the *work* that He has set before us.

As you have read this book, have you found yourself saying, "Yes, that's an issue I need to deal with"? Have you felt a stirring in your spirit that there are things God desires for you to identify, confront, and change in your life?

Act on what God is revealing to you! Get into God's Word and discover the fullness of His answers for your problems, His direction for your future, His desire for your life. Turn His Word into the "work" that prepares you to move into the fullness of all His promises and blessings.

God will help you and God will reward you in this. Of that I am whole-heartedly confident!

APPENDIX

SCRIPTURE REFERENCES ABOUT THE
WOMEN IN *DEAL WITH IT*

CHAPTER I: RUTH
Ruth 1:16–22

But Ruth said:
"Entreat me not to leave you,
Or to turn back from following after you;
For wherever you go, I will go;
And wherever you lodge, I will lodge;
Your people shall be my people,
And your God, my God.
Where you die, I will die,
And there will I be buried.
The LORD do so to me, and more also,
If anything but death parts you and me."

When she [Naomi] saw that she [Ruth] was determined to go with
her, she stopped speaking to her.

Now the two of them went until they came to Bethlehem. And

it happened, when they had come to Bethlehem, that all the city was excited because of them; and the women said, "Is this Naomi?"

But she said to them, "Do not call me Naomi; call me Mara, for the Almighty has dealt very bitterly with me. I went out full, and the LORD has brought me home again empty. Why do you call me Naomi, since the LORD has testified against me, and the Almighty has afflicted me?"

So Naomi returned, and Ruth the Moabitess her daughter-in-law with her, who returned from the country of Moab. Now they came to Bethlehem at the beginning of barley harvest.

CHAPTER 2: LEAH
Genesis 29:15–35

Then Laban said to Jacob, "Because you are my relative, should you therefore serve me for nothing? Tell me, what should your wages be?"

Now Laban had two daughters: the name of the elder was Leah, and the name of the younger was Rachel. Leah's eyes were delicate, but Rachel was beautiful of form and appearance.

Now Jacob loved Rachel; so he said, "I will serve you seven years for Rachel your younger daughter."

And Laban said, "It is better that I give her to you than that I should give her to another man. Stay with me." So Jacob served seven years for Rachel, and they seemed only a few days to him because of the love he had for her.

Then Jacob said to Laban, "Give me my wife, for my days are fulfilled, that I may go in to her." And Laban gathered together all the men of the place and made a feast. Now it came to pass in the evening, that he took Leah his daughter and brought her to Jacob; and he went in to her. And Laban gave his maid Zilpah to his daughter Leah as a maid. So it came to pass in the morning, that behold, it was Leah. And he said to Laban, "What is this you have done to me? Was it not for Rachel that I served you? Why then have you deceived me?"

And Laban said, "It must not be done so in our country, to give the younger before the firstborn. Fulfill her week, and we will give you this one also for the service which you will serve with me still another seven years."

Then Jacob did so and fulfilled her week. So he gave him his daughter Rachel as wife also. And Laban gave his maid Bilhah to his daughter Rachel as a maid. Then Jacob also went in to Rachel, and he also loved Rachel more than Leah. And he served with Laban still another seven years.

When the LORD saw that Leah was unloved, He opened her womb; but Rachel was barren. So Leah conceived and bore a son, and she called his name Reuben; for she said, "The LORD has surely looked on my affliction. Now therefore, my husband will love me." Then she conceived again and bore a son, and said, "Because the LORD has heard that I am unloved, He has therefore given me this son also." And she called his name Simeon. She conceived again and bore a son, and said, "Now this time my husband will become attached to me, because I have borne him three sons." Therefore his name was called Levi. And she conceived again and bore a son, and said, "Now I will praise the LORD." Therefore she called his name Judah. Then she stopped bearing.

CHAPTER 3: RAHAB
    Joshua 2:12–20

[Rahab said:] "Now therefore, I beg you, swear to me by the LORD, since I have shown you kindness, that you also will show kindness to my father's house, and give me a true token, and spare my father, my mother, my brothers, my sisters, and all that they have, and deliver our lives from death."

So the men answered her, "Our lives for yours, if none of you tell this business of ours. And it shall be, when the LORD has given us the land, that we will deal kindly and truly with you."

Then she let them down by a rope through the window, for her house was on the city wall; she dwelt on the wall. And she said to them, "Get to the mountain, lest the pursuers meet you. Hide there three days, until the pursuers have returned. Afterward you may go your way."

So the men said to her: "We will be blameless of this oath of yours which you have made us swear, unless, when we come into the land, you bind this line of scarlet cord in the window through which you let us down, and unless you bring your father, your mother, your brothers, and all your father's household to your own home. So it shall be that whoever goes outside the doors of your house into the street, his blood shall be on his own head, and we will be guiltless. And whoever is with you in the house, his blood shall be on our head if a hand is laid on him. And if you tell this business of ours, then we will be free from your oath which you made us swear."

CHAPTER 4: DORCAS
Acts 9:36–42

At Joppa there was a certain disciple named Tabitha, which is translated Dorcas. This woman was full of good works and charitable deeds which she did. But it happened in those days that she became sick and died. When they had washed her, they laid her in an upper room. And since Lydda was near Joppa, and the disciples had heard that Peter was there, they sent two men to him, imploring him not to delay in coming to them. Then Peter arose and went with them. When he had come, they brought him to the upper room. And all the widows stood by him weeping, showing the tunics and garments which Dorcas had made while she was with them. But Peter put them all out, and knelt down and prayed. And turning to the body he said, "Tabitha, arise." And she opened her eyes, and when she saw Peter she sat up. Then he gave her his hand and lifted her up; and when he had called the saints and widows, he presented her alive. And it became known throughout all Joppa, and many believed on the Lord.

CHAPTER 5: GOMER
Hosea 1:2–3

When the LORD began to speak by Hosea, the LORD said to Hosea: "Go, take yourself a wife of harlotry, and children of harlotry, for the land has committed great harlotry by departing from the LORD." So he went and took Gomer the daughter of Diblaim, and she conceived and bore him a son.

Hosea 2:4–5

"I will not have mercy on her children, for they are the children of harlotry. For their mother has played the harlot; she who conceived them has behaved shamefully. For she said, 'I will go after my lovers, who give me my bread and my water, my wool and my linen, my oil and my drink.'"

Hosea 3:1–3

Then the LORD said to me, "Go again, love a woman who is loved by a lover and is committing adultery, just like the love of the LORD for the children of Israel, who look to other gods and love the raisin cakes of the pagans." So I bought her for myself for fifteen shekels of silver, and one and one-half homers of barley. And I said to her, "You shall stay with me many days; you shall not play the harlot, nor shall you have a man—so, too, will I be toward you."

CHAPTER 6: HANNAH
1 Samuel 1:1–20

Now there was a certain man of Ramathaim Zophim, of the mountains of Ephraim, and his name was Elkanah the son of Jeroham, the son of Elihu, the son of Tohu, the son of Zuph, an Ephraimite. And he had two wives: the name of one was Hannah, and the name of the other Peninnah. Peninnah had children, but Hannah had no children. This man went up from his city yearly to worship and sacrifice to the LORD of hosts in Shiloh. Also the two sons of Eli, Hophni and Phinehas, the priests of the LORD, were there. And whenever the time came for Elkanah to make an offering, he would give portions to Peninnah his wife and to all her sons and daughters. But to Hannah he would give a double portion, for he loved Hannah, although the LORD had closed her womb. And her rival also provoked her severely, to make her miserable, because the LORD had closed her womb. So it was, year by year, when she went up to the house of the LORD, that she provoked her; therefore she wept and did not eat.

Then Elkanah her husband said to her, "Hannah, why do you weep? Why do you not eat? And why is your heart grieved? Am I not better to you than ten sons?"

So Hannah arose after they had finished eating and drinking in Shiloh. Now Eli the priest was sitting on the seat by the doorpost of the tabernacle of the LORD. And she was in bitterness of soul, and prayed to the LORD and wept in anguish. Then she made a vow and said, "O LORD of hosts, if You will indeed look on the affliction of Your maidservant and remember me, and not forget Your maidservant, but will give Your maidservant a male child, then I will give him to the LORD all the days of his life, and no razor shall come upon his head."

And it happened, as she continued praying before the LORD, that

Eli watched her mouth. Now Hannah spoke in her heart; only her lips moved, but her voice was not heard. Therefore Eli thought she was drunk. So Eli said to her, "How long will you be drunk? Put your wine away from you!"

But Hannah answered and said, "No, my lord, I am a woman of sorrowful spirit. I have drunk neither wine nor intoxicating drink, but have poured out my soul before the LORD. Do not consider your maidservant a wicked woman, for out of the abundance of my complaint and grief I have spoken until now."

Then Eli answered and said, "Go in peace, and the God of Israel grant your petition which you have asked of Him."

And she said, "Let your maidservant find favor in your sight." So the woman went her way and ate, and her face was no longer sad.

Then they rose early in the morning and worshiped before the LORD, and returned and came to their house at Ramah. And Elkanah knew Hannah his wife, and the LORD remembered her. So it came to pass in the process of time that Hannah conceived and bore a son, and called his name Samuel, saying, "Because I have asked for him from the LORD."

CHAPTER 7: MARY MAGDALENE
John 20:1–3, 10–14

Now the first day of the week Mary Magdalene went to the tomb early, while it was still dark, and saw that the stone had been taken away from the tomb. Then she ran and came to Simon Peter, and to the other disciple, whom Jesus loved, and said to them, "They have taken away the Lord out of the tomb, and we do not know where they have laid Him." Peter therefore went out, and the other disciple, and were going to the tomb. . . . Then the disciples went away again to their own homes.

But Mary stood outside by the tomb weeping, and as she wept she stooped down and looked into the tomb. And she saw two angels in white sitting, one at the head and the other at the feet, where the body of Jesus had lain. Then they said to her, "Woman, why are you weeping?" She said to them, "Because they have taken away my Lord, and I do not know where they have laid Him." Now when she had said this, she turned around and saw Jesus standing there, and did not know that it was Jesus.

CHAPTER 8: THE SHUNAMMITE WOMAN
   2 Kings 4:8–10

Now it happened one day that Elisha went to Shunem, where there was a notable woman, and she persuaded him to eat some food. So it was, as often as he passed by, he would turn in there to eat some food. And she said to her husband, "Look now, I know that this is a holy man of God, who passes by us regularly. Please, let us make a small upper room on the wall; and let us put a bed for him there, and a table and a chair and a lampstand; so it will be, whenever he comes to us, he can turn in there."

   2 Kings 4:14–17

So he [Elisha] said, "What then is to be done for her?" And Gehazi answered, "Actually, she has no son, and her husband is old."

So he said, "Call her." When he had called her, she stood in the doorway. Then he said, "About this time next year you shall embrace a son." And she said, "No, my lord. Man of God, do not lie to your maidservant!"

But the woman conceived, and bore a son when the appointed time had come, of which Elisha had told her.

CHAPTER 9: THE DAUGHTERS OF ZELOPHEHAD
Numbers 27:1–7

Then came the daughters of Zelophehad the son of Hepher, the son of Gilead, the son of Machir, the son of Manasseh, from the families of Manasseh the son of Joseph; and these were the names of his daughters: Mahlah, Noah, Hoglah, Milcah, and Tirzah. And they stood before Moses, before Eleazar the priest, and before the leaders and all the congregation by the doorway of the tabernacle of meeting, saying: "Our father died in the wilderness; but he was not in the company of those who gathered together against the LORD, in company with Korah, but he died in his own sin; and he had no sons. Why should the name of our father be removed from among his family because he had no son? Give us a possession among our father's brothers."

So Moses brought their case before the LORD.

And the LORD spoke to Moses, saying, "The daughters of Zelophehad speak what is right; you shall surely give them a possession of inheritance among their father's brothers, and cause the inheritance of their father to pass to them."

CHAPTER 10: ESTHER
Esther 4:13–14

And Mordecai told them to answer Esther: "Do not think in your heart that you will escape in the king's palace any more than all the other Jews. For if you remain completely silent at this time, relief and deliverance will arise for the Jews from another place, but you and your father's house will perish. Yet who knows whether you have come to the kingdom for such a time as this?"

ABOUT THE AUTHOR

PAULA WHITE, pastor, teacher, and speaker, is known for her dynamic Bible teaching and preaching with delivery as an exhorter and motivator. She is also the host of the nationally syndicated program, *Paula White Today,* seen on BET, TBN, Church Channel, Word Network, Court TV, Miracle Network, Daystar Television Network, as well as many other stations. With a message that crosses denominational, cultural, and economic barriers, this wife, mother, preacher, administrator, humanitarian, and evangelist is also the copastor and cofounder of Without Walls International Church. Together with her husband, Dr. Randy White, they pastor a thriving, multiracial congregation of some 15,000 in Tampa, Florida, one of the fastest growing churches of its kind in the country.